A Bend in the Road
Is Not the
End of the Road

ALSO BY JOAN LUNDEN

Joan Lunden's Healthy Cooking with Laura Morton

Joan Lunden's Healthy Living: A Practical, Inspirational Guide to Creating Balance in Your Life with Laura Morton

Good Morning, I'm Joan Lunden with Ardy Friedberg

Joan Lunden's

A Bend in the Road
Is Not the
End of the Road

10 POSITIVE PRINCIPLES
FOR DEALING WITH CHANGE

Joan Lunden
and Andrea Cagan

WILLIAM MORROW AND COMPANY, INC./ NEW YORK

Grateful acknowledgment is made for permission to reprint excerpts from the following:
"Hero," courtesy of Columbia Records, written by Mariah Carey and Walter Afanasieff;
"Gotta Be," courtesy of Sony 550 Music; "Because You Loved Me," words and music
by Diane Warren, © 1996 REALSONGS (ASCAP) and TOUCHSTONE PICTURES
SONGS & MUSIC, INC. (ASCAP). All Rights Reserved. Used by Permission.
WARNER BROS. PUBLICATIONS U.S. INC., Miami, FL 33014.

It is the policy of William Morrow and Company, Inc., and its imprints and affiliates,
recognizing the importance of preserving what has been written,
to print the books we publish on acid-free paper,
and we exert our best efforts to that end.

Library of Congress Cataloging-in-Publication Data

Lunden, Joan.
    [Bend in the road is not the end of the road]
    Joan Lunden's a bend in the road is not the end of the road : 10
positive principles for dealing with change / Joan Lunden and Andrea
Cagan.
      p.   cm.
    ISBN 0-688-16083-2
    1. Change (Psychology)   I. Cagan, Andrea.   II. Title.
BF637.C4L86 1998
155.2'4—dc21   98-27579
                                                      CIP

Printed in the United States of America

First Edition

1 2 3 4 5 6 7 8 9 10

Book Design and Composition by Pauline Neuwirth, Neuwirth & Associates, Inc.

www.williammorrow.com

Dedication

Ralph Waldo Emerson once said, "Self-trust is the first secret of success."
However, even the most optimistic person needs a little encouragement from
time to time to maintain that self-trust. This is especially true when life throws us
a curve, or when we're venturing into new, unknown territory.

I rounded the latest bend in my road with a wonderful partner in life, Jeff
Konigsberg, to whom I dedicate this book. Whenever my heart was heavy, he
could lift my spirits; when my self-confidence would waver, he would remind
me of my accomplishments and my opportunities. He believed in me so completely that it helped me believe in myself. Just knowing that I had his uncon-
ditional love, no matter what was around the bend, gave me comfort and
strength.

I also dedicate this book to my three daughters, Jamie, Lindsay, and Sarah.
They were all born during my tenure at *Good Morning America*, so they have
grown up with the unique demands and pressures of public life. Having the
opportunity this past year to wake up with them in the mornings and more
time to share in their lives has been a joy beyond words. It also opened my
eyes to how much they sacrificed and persevered under those extraordinary
demands. I am so very proud of the people they are becoming.

And finally, when we watch our children evolve and see the foundations
we've laid begin to take shape, we are reminded of our own foundations. My
mom and dad, Gladyce and Erle, laid solid foundations for me and my brother, Jeff. I am grateful for that, and I constantly call upon their wisdom and
guidance as you will see throughout this book.

Acknowledgments

The idea for this book was born out of a real-life bend in my road. I'd like to thank some special people in my life who helped me around this bend and who helped make this book possible.

It goes without saying that those closest to us must be generous enough to allow us the time and space to write. Jeff and my girls, Jamie, Lindsay, and Sarah, were incredibly understanding throughout this project and supported me as I rounded this bend. I am thankful to them.

Another person who seems to spend almost as much time with me as my family is Jill Seigerman. She began working for me at about the same time that the press decided they would follow my every move (not to mention a few moves I didn't make). She has often been the calm in the middle of my stormy days. In three years she has certainly been there for many bends in the road. I thank her for her loyalty, her impeccable sensibility, her drive and enthusiasm, and her dedication in the midst of much change. I hope that we work together for many years to come. Oh, I also thank her husband, Evan, for his generosity, sacrifice, and support on the days and weeks on the road and late nights.

I want to also thank a dear friend, confidant, and sage adviser, my attorney Marc Chamlin. He's been through a lot of change with me over the past two decades—some terrifically exciting and some tumultuous. I can always trust that Marc's wise advice will help keep me on the high road. He is always fair and never fuels a fire. He tells me what I need to hear, not just what I may want to hear. I consider myself most fortunate to have Marc there with me helping me navigate my path.

Acknowledgments

The last twenty years of my career have been more than one could ever hope for and I owe a tremendous amount of thanks to Jim Griffin at the William Morris Agency. I thank him for his support, guidance, and perseverance.

When we experience change, we all need to expand our vision of ourselves. When it came time to expand my vision, I looked to Debra Goldfarb and Lee Gabler at Creative Artists Agency. They helped me forge my new path and reinvent my life.

Expanding my career to include writing books has been incredibly rewarding. Al Lowman has shown amazing enthusiasm for my writing. He definitely fuels my passion to continue sharing. He also paired me with Andrea Cagan, my coauthor, who worked diligently at keeping me focused, open, always reaching and digging deeper. We both had opportunities to help each other deal with change while writing about that very subject.

At William Morrow, I found a wonderful home for this book. I thank Meaghan Dowling for her wisdom and guidance. I'd also like to acknowledge the efforts of Betty Kelly, editor in chief, William Morrow; Paul Fedorko, former publisher, William Morrow; and Ellen Levine, editor in chief, *Good Housekeeping*, in making this book possible from the start.

When it comes to making the right decisions with respect to the press, you can't ask for anyone better than Stan Rosenfield. He not only helps me keep things in perspective but helps me approach everything with a sense of humor. (And sometimes you need a sense of humor when dealing with the tabloids!)

I take my hat off to the tireless efforts of Anne Marie Riccitelli—whose impeccable press and public-relations instincts never cease to amaze me. She worked hard to steer me in the right direction and always went the extra mile.

Also at ABC, Ida Astute always came to my rescue, making photo editing a snap! She is responsible for many of the photos in this book.

Danielle Paltrowitz has worked day in and day out on the many details that go into making a book like this possible. Kristen Barry makes my hair worth photographing and Michelle Cutler puts on my happy face. They are both artists whom I greatly appreciate, not only for their talent but for their loyalty as well.

I'd like to thank several close friends who have been there with me through many real life changes and have also been helpful in writing this book. Elise Silvestri and Scot Evans are like family to me—they've been remarkable listeners and given sound advice. Friend, confidant, and trainer, Barbara Brandt is not only a good example of how to exercise and eat right but also exemplifies living each day to the fullest—continuing to challenge and reinvent herself and, just as important, reminding all of us not to sweat the small stuff.

Ellen McGrath and Pat Manocchia both dedicate themselves to helping us take charge of our health and our happiness. I want to thank them for the time they gave to help me with this book, as well as the friendship and advice they have given me personally.

Eric Schotz and Bill Palentonio have provided me with many "opportunities for growth" with their wacky—er, I mean brilliant ideas for my "Behind Closed Doors" segments. Whether soaring in a U2, diving in a nuclear sub, or strutting as a showgirl, I've always had to stretch further than I thought I could. For these layers of growth, self-confidence, and life fulfillment, I thank them.

And now, when it comes to the bottom line, I want to thank my accountant, Richard Koenigsberg, and my financial adviser, David Harris, for teaching me how to take control of my bottom line. That was one of the big steps I had to take to make it successfully around this bend. They empowered me to take control of my finances rather than to fear them.

And finally I'd like to thank each and every one of you who motivate me to continue on this path. See you around the other side of the bend!

Contents

Bends in the Road

Change What You Can, Accept What You Can't

> When we can no longer change
> a situation, we are challenged to
> change ourselves.
>
> —Victor Frankel

It was Wednesday, May 7, 1997. I awoke with a start, and looked at the alarm clock—3:45 A.M. For almost twenty years, as cohost of *Good Morning America*, my mornings had begun this way. Why, after all these years, could my body never get used to this schedule? Of course, this was an exceptionally hectic and trying week. The show was in upheaval and, for the first time, its ratings were slipping. Rumors were rampant that one or all of us would be replaced. Each morning, along with our script, we could count on at least one news article predicting who was taking our jobs. Through all of this, our lives had to go on as usual.

For me, that meant the release of my latest book, *Joan Lunden's Healthy Living*, and all the promotion that went along with its publication: media interviews and book signings. In addition, I had a photo shoot for the upcoming June cover of *TV Guide*. In the darkness, I pulled myself out of my warm bed and shuffled across the carpet to the bathroom. The early-morning wake-ups seemed so much more difficult these days. I didn't know whether it was from trying to stay up with my teenage daughters at night, dealing with the chronic problems of *GMA* during the day, or just the inevitable toll of years of constant sleep deprivation.

"God, I wish these early mornings could end," I quietly sighed to myself as I turned on the shower. Somehow the water beating down over my body could always wash away the exhaustion enough to get me through another day.

Immediately following the show that morning, I was scheduled to sit down for the interview that would accompany the upcoming *TV Guide* cover. The writer, Janice Kaplan, had worked with me over the years and had become a friend. But I knew that for this interview, she was doing her job for *TV Guide*. That job was to extract as much as possible about the fate of *Good Morning America* and, more specifically, my role on the show. Were any of the rumors true? Was I leaving or being pushed out? How was I dealing with that prospect? How would I feel about their grooming somebody to take my place? Then there would be the questions about every aspect of my personal life. Janice would be searching for *any* details about the man in my life, Jeff Konigsberg. Even though we'd only been dating six months, I knew there would be the inevitable "Do you have any wedding plans?" question.

Before the interview, I called my agent to find out if the ABC executives had made any decisions about *GMA* and my future role with the network. "Are they close to making a move yet?" I asked. "This is *TV Guide*," I reminded him. "They're pros. The writer is going to ask me all the hard questions. If the ABC executives know anything at all, I wish they would please help me out here."

My agent sensed my frustration. We had asked ABC, in our last contract negotiations, to move me out of the early-morning slot and into prime time. They insisted they weren't yet ready to make a change. I agreed to stay for at least another two years while they formulated their plan for the next generation of *GMA*. Then, almost before the ink dried on that contract, they started talking to other candidates for my job. Since viewers weren't aware of my negotiations, the network had created a situation where it looked like I was being shoved out. It was not a comfortable place to be, and there was nothing I could do about it.

"Sorry, Joan," he said. "They're just not sure what they're going to do yet."

Well, I knew what *I* had to do—get myself prepared for the interview. First I conferred with Stan Rosenfield, my public-relations adviser over the years, to discuss the overall tone of the interview. Anne Marie Riccitelli, who, at the time, was the executive director of publicity for ABC-TV, rehearsed with me before the interview, as we always did. She conjured up two pages of questions, making them as tough and cutting as she could. "Don't let her get your hackles up," she reminded me, "no matter what she asks."

The whole interview was a bit strained. In addition to the *GMA* turmoil, Jeff was accompanying me on this interview at *TV Guide*'s request,

Jeff always has a supportive arm around me—here on vacation in Kona, Hawaii.

and I was nervous about how he would feel when asked personal questions about our relationship and about his being younger than I (a guaranteed question).

It would be interesting to see how they would incorporate the *Good Morning America* politics into an issue devoted to spring fitness and the people on television who inspire it. During the photo session, they had requested that I wear workout clothes while flexing my biceps with ten-pound free weights. Trying to be a good sport, I had chosen one of the spandex outfits their stylist had brought along, picked up the weights, flexed, and flashed a warm smile at the photographer's lens.

I was already imagining the headline: LUNDEN FLEXES HER MUSCLES IN THE MORNING BATTLE FOR RATINGS.

Despite the tension, chaos, and turmoil at *GMA*, and my desire to let a relationship with a man I deeply cared about grow naturally, I managed to get through the interview. As predicted, though, Janice asked all the hard questions: "Joan, you've hosted *Good Morning America* for seventeen years. How will you feel if they take you off the program?"

"Janice, I'm sure I'd have a little bit of a funny feeling," I said, "since I'd be leaving my security blanket where I know what I'm doing. But I'd also welcome the opportunity in a new arena."

"But wouldn't you be resentful if you still had to prove yourself after two decades with the network?"

"It would be up to me to be creative and tenacious," I said. "When I first got to *GMA*, I was always given small stories, but I knew that instead of being discouraged, I should make each one shine. Well, I can still use that philosophy. I just want a venue in which to flourish."

"The network hired Elizabeth Vargas and it's rumored they've talked to several other young anchors around the country. It appears that ABC wants to find a younger host."

"I can't tell you what's on the minds of the ABC executives or what their plan is. You can dissect it and analyze it all you want, but I plan to focus on the good part—which would be an opportunity in a new time period."

"But aren't you going through some moments of self-doubt? Isn't it natural to feel some hurt when you consider the possibility of being replaced?"

Jeff spoke up. "Absolutely not. Whatever happens, there would be no sense of failure here. I've seen the impact Joan has on people and that wouldn't change. Joan would just go on."

She turned back to me. "After years of insisting you have the best job in the world, how would you adjust to not being on TV every morning?" she asked.

"If I left *GMA* tomorrow, if I never worked another day in TV and just spent my time writing and doing all the other things I want, it would be okay," I said. "Plus, I have another life at home with my daughters that's full and a top priority. People think that as children get older, they need less. That may be true in terms of watching them, but otherwise it gets much harder. It's not just lip service to say that I really want a chance to be around more."

"What would you do next?" Janice wanted to know.

"The fact is that I've never been so open-minded about my future." I looked at Jeff and smiled. "Maybe it's because I've really enjoyed my life in the last year."

"What's it like being with a younger man?"

"Our philosophies and moral fiber are the same. We're really, really happy and we spend a lot of time together. People say we're very similar, and that's important when you're talking about a lifetime mate. We talk about the future, but we have to let that happen."

Janice kept on plugging away. "It certainly feels like you're being nudged out of your long-held TV spot, Joan."

"Actually, I feel like I'm sitting in the catbird seat. I could decide to be at home more with my kids while I'm doing my specials. I could do other shows at ABC. Or I could sign with somebody else to do a completely different kind of show."

"What if they actually *do* hire somebody younger than you to take your seat after you've been there for so long?"

Again, she was referring to the rumors that the thirty-five-year-old new-comer, Elizabeth Vargas, was being groomed to take my place. ABC had recently hired Elizabeth to be the newsreader for *GMA*. With her arrival came rumors that she was my likely successor, and of course, the critics automatically assumed that she and I didn't get along. Media reports indicated that I might be pulled from the show, and *TV Guide* had run a Lunden vs. Vargas piece entitled "Showdown at Sunrise." The various

Me with Elizabeth Vargas on the GMA *set—February 1997.*

tabloid articles that emerged began with speculation about a tense relationship and escalated to reports of a knock-down, drag-out catfight.
While the "catfight" was a figment of their imagination, the media were
correct in their sense that something was afoot with the network.

"You know, Janice, who will come after me is not for me to figure out,
but I would hope they'd make a good choice. Even if I wasn't there, I
wouldn't want to see the show fail. I have twenty years invested in this
franchise."

With the interview ended, Jeff and I left the city, picked up the girls from
school, and headed home. As I entered my house, the phone was ringing.
It was my attorney, Marc Chamlin, and my agent, Jim Griffin.

"Joni," Marc said, "we have something to talk to you about."

As soon as I heard his calm, reserved tone, I knew what had happened.

"ABC has finally decided to make the change," Marc went on. "They think the time has come to revamp *Good Morning America*. We have some talking to do about what your role will be with the network, since they're hiring another host to take your place in September."

The words echoed in my ears as if in slow motion. T-h-e-y-'r-e h-i-r-i-n-g s-o-m-e-o-n-e t-o t-a-k-e y-o-u-r p-l-a-c-e. I knew in my heart it was time for a change. I'd been talking about it for over a year, and the press had been speculating about it for months. However, nothing could have adequately prepared me for the shock of this phone call.

The impact of the change I would be facing was immense; it wasn't just my job that would change but my entire lifestyle. It's true, I had asked for it, I wanted to be able to spend more time with my girls, more time with Jeff, and I wanted to live a "normal" life. But such an enormous transition seemed like a scary proposition. Not knowing exactly what I would be doing made me uneasy. Yes, I knew it was time to move on, but on to what? What would my life be like? What would I do with my time? They say you're only as good as your last show. Could I leave a daily show and work in prime-time specials, or did I need to jump right into another daily show? What kind of show? Would it mean changing networks? There were such big questions to face.

I felt a numbness, then a tightening in my neck and stomach as a thousand disjointed thoughts raced through my mind and a mixture of conflicting emotions washed over me. What were my opportunities once I was off *GMA*? Would all those years of early mornings pay off, or would I be a has-been? If I tried something else, would I be good at it? Would I like my "new life"? Would I still be able to live in the same way? This couldn't be happening—not to me or my girls. Would I still be able to support my teenage daughters? What about my lifestyle? My identity? My house? I better sell it fast, and downsize . . .

How fast we can spin a negative web, if we let ourselves —a web that doesn't let us think clearly.

I tried to refocus on the conversation and how the situation was going to develop. "Why September?" I asked quickly. "Why don't they just go ahead and make the change now?" It was May, and I thought it would be extremely difficult to be on the air through the entire summer, knowing I would be leaving in the fall. Couldn't we just go ahead and get it over with?

"They're still not ready for you to go yet," said my agent, Jim. "They don't even know who your replacement is going to be. They're just letting you know that now, they're committed to making the change. Remember, though, you're secure at the network," he continued.

"You signed a three-year contract two months ago," Marc chimed in. "Joni, this is the call you've been waiting for. Are you forgetting that last year, we were badgering them to let you off this early schedule and move you to prime time? You're the one who asked for this, and now, you're getting exactly what you wanted, exactly what you've been wishing for."

I could hardly hear what they were saying. You know the old adage, "Be careful what you wish for; you might get it." It's often said that not getting what you desire and getting what you desire can be equally disappointing.

Despite the fact that I had planted the seed of this change myself, I couldn't help but feel that someone "out there" was taking something away from me, and taking *me* away from millions of viewers who had counted on me to be there each morning when their alarm clocks went off. I was the one greeting them when they pulled themselves out of their toasty beds each morning, putting one foot, then the other, out onto the cold floor, rubbing their eyes, and letting my smile and my voice usher them into another day. Day after day, year after year, I had helped them set the mood for the day, offering my "morning friends" the latest happenings in virtually every field. I felt a unique closeness with my viewers and it was hard to imagine parting with them.

Even though it always seems as though change comes as an unexpected shock, more often than not, there are warning signs along the way. For all of us at *Good Morning America*, it was when the program was taken over by the news division. ABC News had been wanting control of *GMA* for years. When they finally took it over, one executive said, "This show has been number one in the morning ratings for the past seventeen years. You know what they say: If it ain't broke, don't fix it." But it wasn't long before changes did start to happen. First a new logo, then new music, new graphics, new colors, new contributors, and a new set. Then another news executive was heard to say, "We don't understand the show. It's not really a news show—it has celebrities, bands, and cooking spots . . . "

That's what all of us had been saying for years. The show is more than just news. It is unique, and that's why the network programmers back in the seventies put it in the entertainment division and not the news division. So why change the show? At that moment I should have recognized the handwriting on the wall.

Stop! Wait a minute! Aren't I the author of *Joan Lunden's Healthy Living*, a book about how to consciously create peace and tranquillity in your life? I had written that we should be nonreactive in crisis. Stay positive, calm, and focused. There are a lot of things in life over which we have little or no control. But that doesn't mean we have to be victims. We can learn to work with these new forces, understand them, and use their energies to increase our strength, wisdom, and compassion.

Yes, that was me, and as much as I knew I shouldn't be allowing it, the human emotions of fear, anger, and resentment were forcing their way into my head and rushing throughout my entire body. That's why my attorney was purposely using such a calm, reassuring voice.

It was time to follow my own advice: *Change what you can and accept what you can't.* I took a long, deep breath. I knew that was the first step to clearing my head of all the mind chatter—the negative, unproductive thoughts that were causing my muscles to tighten and obstructing my ability to think calmly. As the new air filled my lungs, my mind slowed down and started to think rationally. Could I stop long enough to hear the good part of this call, or was I going to obsess that someone else would be filling the seat I had filled for all these years?

"Exactly what does this mean?" I asked Jim, ready to shift my focus.

"You're finally getting off the early-morning schedule," Jim repeated. "Do you hear me, Joan? No more early-morning wake-up calls."

I felt the panic start to ease, the dead, empty feeling in the pit of my stomach slowly start to let go. I thought back to some months earlier, when we had completed negotiating my current contract. In past years, as soon as I signed a contract, I had been able to rationalize the crazy schedule by thinking, "Hey, I'd much rather have this schedule than a nine-to-five, because at least I have a good part of my days to myself. Granted, with my early call, they're long days. But it's a trade-off." Okay, so it was a good rationalization.

I knew I was fortunate to have such a great job, but over the last year, the compromises that were required in my personal life in order to maintain that job had become daunting. I always loved my job once I got there, but I was tired of my career taking such a toll on me and my family. I needed my life back. Just before I signed this last contract, I remember saying to my attorney, "I don't feel good about this. I just don't know if I can actually put pen to paper and sign back on to this grind, sacrificing my life and my time with my kids, never being available to my friends or myself." I reluctantly signed the new contract, which was to begin in February of 1997, that would bind me to the early-morning schedule for two or possibly three more years. Although they had upped the ante to an offer too good to refuse, I felt uncharacteristically troubled, a feeling that did not leave the next day. In fact, it never left me.

During this time, I found a postcard that so reminded me of my contract negotiations with ABC, I kept it on my desk. The postcard was a black and white drawing of a man and a dog. The man has a stick in his hand that he's just getting ready to throw for the dog to fetch. The caption above the dog says, "OK, just one more and then I've got to get on with my life." I felt like that dog, and the network executives had made the stick look so appealing, how could I possibly not go for it? I had agreed to stay on, but part of me was thinking, "Okay, throw the stick for one more contract and I'll get it, but then I have to get on with my life." It made me smile, and even laugh, at something that was otherwise unsettling.

For most of my career, I had bounded out of bed at the ungodly hour of 3:45 A.M. ready to face the day. But lately, it seemed like my rhythms had

shifted. I was staying up later, attempting to be more "normal," and as a result, I often found myself sleeping through my second alarm, giving myself a bashing headache by leaping out of bed when the ABC driver knocked at the front door. Deep inside, although I hated to admit it to myself, I knew that it was time for a change. But since I was supporting three daughters, a few more years of security had their appeal. Like most people, I was resisting change, which is a natural reaction.

We cannot avoid change. It is the one constant in our lives, yet it produces the greatest amount of fear. But when you examine the fear of change, it's really only worry about events that *might* happen in the future. Isn't that a little like making payments on a debt you haven't yet incurred? It reminds me of Mark Twain's great line: "I have been through some terrible things in my life, some of which actually happened."

Looking back, I see that any smart businessperson would know that if you've stayed in the same place for twenty years, you should be thinking about stretching and making a change. So, although I hadn't necessarily allowed the thought to reside in the forefront of my brain, intellectually, I knew a change was imminent. For the past five years, I'd felt like I was preparing for that change, but I didn't necessarily know what it would look like. This phone call was the first step.

During the remainder of the call, I focused on where this new path might be leading me, rather than allowing the sudden fear of change to paralyze me and cloud my vision. I needed to harness my belief in myself to give me strength and energy to focus on the road ahead. I remembered back to the day when ABC News took over *Good Morning America* from the network's entertainment division and everyone who worked on the show was worried. What was going to happen? Would they change the show? Would that hurt our ratings? And, of course, who would be fired first? I left that meeting and walked upstairs to my dressing room for an attitude check. I happened to pick up an inspirational book I had just started reading: *Wherever You Go, There You Are* by Jon Kabat-Zinn. The book literally fell open to a chapter entitled "You Can't Stop the Waves, But You Can Learn to Surf."

What did it mean? Simply put, when we can no longer change a situation, we are challenged to change ourselves. When change comes, it's natural to get upset and uptight, and then to start building your case and getting defensive. Of course, nothing good can come from this kind of negative thinking. Learning to surf means riding the wave, transcending the change, and being able to create meaning and purpose from whatever life has in store for you. It means being able to calmly survey all your options and learning to work with those that will serve you best in the end. It means letting go of resistance in order to let in all sorts of new possibilities. Embracing this philosophy allows you to act out of strength, not weakness. I could calmly and productively craft my response to these new bosses. This was a defining moment and I knew it. I needed to stay on top of the wave, head up high, shoulders relaxed, knees absorbing the shock. I needed to surf.

Now, two years later, I was surfing once again. But this time, I felt like I was riding the biggest wave yet. When I hung up the phone, Jeff sat down beside me.

"Joan, are you okay? Do you want to talk about it?" he asked, always ready to support me whenever I need it.

"Actually, I think I need to take a step back and let all this sink in." Really, I was afraid to talk about it because I didn't want to break down. When I had talked with the network during negotiations about moving on, it all seemed so far off and so natural. Now that it was happening, it all seemed quite jarring. All of a sudden, the reality of the change crystallized and seemed so real, so big, so fast, and so sad. I didn't think it would feel so sad.

My mind raced the rest of the day, as it tried to catch up with the reality of this news. I needed to absorb the enormity of the transition I was facing. I didn't sleep much that night and I went in to work the next morning unrested and restless, with a torturous secret. I was uneasy on the inside, but I tried to keep a relaxed face on the outside. I was unusually quiet as I sat in the makeup chair that morning. In fact, I was worried that my colleagues might suspect that something was wrong.

There was one person I would tell almost immediately: Charlie Gibson, my ten-year cohost on *GMA* and my good friend. We were like brother and sister, and it didn't feel right keeping this information from him, since it would be affecting him as well. "I need to talk to you, Charlie, in private." I followed him down the hall to his dressing room with a very strange feeling, knowing that I had news that was so enormous, it would affect the future of both of our lives. When we stepped inside, I could hear the door close with a bang that was louder than life.

Me with Charlie Gibson—the best teammate in the world.

"It's happening, Charlie. ABC is redesigning the show and they've finally decided to make the change. I'll be leaving the show, come September fifth."

"You're kidding, right?"

"No, I'm not kidding. They called me yesterday. They're ready to do it."

Charlie got up, put his arms around me, and we hugged for a long

15

time. I'd be lying if I told you that we didn't shed a tear or two. Of course, it didn't really take either of us by surprise; we had both been talking about making this change for about a year now, and there had been rumblings within management for months. They had become particularly loud lately as I went out on my book tour, speaking across the country, appearing on talk shows and doing magazine interviews. Interviews had always been a big part of my job, but I was even more visible than usual. Articles were appearing in newspapers daily speculating about the morning TV network battle. Everyone wanted to know what was happening at *Good Morning America*. I wanted to be able to shut out the constant talk about an inevitable change so I could go about my life normally. But each day, I could hear the door closing on this chapter of my life.

WHEN ONE DOOR CLOSES, ANOTHER OPENS

Particularly poignant for me was an interview I had done with TV host Charlie Rose only a few weeks before the call from ABC. Charlie had said to me, "What will it mean to you if some ABC executive comes to you and says, 'Joan, you have made a huge contribution to *Good Morning America*. I know we just signed a new contract for three years, but we want to change *Good Morning America*'? . . . Do you say, 'Okay, I've got a lot of things to do with my life . . . When a door closes, a window opens'? Or do you say, 'Who the hell are you?' "

I answered, "You really just said it, Charlie. When one door closes, another opens, and if you can keep that attitude, you've really got one of the secrets to happiness in life. I would write them a letter and say, 'Thank you for twenty of the most exciting years, my ticket to adventure.' And if I have self-confidence and self-esteem and I know I do what I do well, then I can take that and move on. Change is necessary for growth."

"So, in a way," he said, "if somebody would come to you and say, 'No *GMA* anymore,' they might be doing you a favor?"

He couldn't have stated it better. But now, faced with the reality of the change, a certain kind of paralysis seemed to take over. Maybe you've felt it when you've gone through some uncomfortable change or challenge in your life. It can be anything from a change in jobs to a breakup with a boyfriend. Even if you have orchestrated the breakup, there's still that scary feeling that your entire life will be different or empty because it will no longer be consumed with that person anymore. I guess that's how I was feeling about my job with *GMA*. Getting the word that they were finally moving forward with this change meant that now I was going to have to deal with it. So I gave myself about twenty-four hours to agonize.

I went from complete numbness to total sadness. In my private moments, I allowed myself to cry, to feel the loss of such an enormous part of my identity and my life as I knew it. This was the only life I had known for twenty years. Now that it was changing, I had to wonder if this was as good as it gets. Maybe this was my best venue, my real niche. Would I ever be able to replicate it and reach higher heights? And after having been with Jeff for only six months, my own insecurities made me wonder how this change would affect our relationship.

As shaky as I felt, I was adamant about restraining myself from showing it to other people. Particularly, my girls. I didn't want them to feel frightened of the future, and I knew if they sensed it in me, they, too,

> *Every adversity, every failure, and every heartbreak carries with it the seed of an equivalent or greater benefit.*
>
> —*Napoleon Hill*

would be fearful. Fortunately, I didn't have much time to indulge myself in despair, because I was scheduled to leave in two days for a weeklong Scandinavian tour with *Good Morning America*.

BROODING
IS NOT AN OPTION

It was May, "Sweeps" month, ratings time for all the networks, and consequently, a time for whirlwind exotic trips. There was always a weeklong adventure to somewhere interesting. Unless you were in a coma or actively throwing up, staying home was not an option. I managed to postpone leaving for one day to address the issue at hand, but even so, I didn't have the luxury of wallowing in my insecurities. Maybe that was a gift—the fact that brooding was not an option. It forced me to call upon all my strength to stay level-headed and look to the future.

I was reminded of my mother and how she had handled traumatic change. When I was twelve, my father flew our private plane from our home in Sacramento to Los Angeles to attend a medical convention. It was a flight that I missed taking with him only by moments. On the way back home, his plane crashed in Malibu Canyon. Our grief was overwhelming, but I remember my mom telling me one day that she had to get out there and take over my father's work. He had been in the midst of building a medical center, a hospital, and several other big projects, and she had to gather her resolve in order to support our family and see my father's dreams come true.

TOP LEFT: *Me at age six with my mom.*
TOP RIGHT: *My brother and me visiting Canada at age ten.*
BOTTOM LEFT: *Me with my family in Squaw Valley, California, for the 1960 Olympics.*
BOTTOM RIGHT: *My mom and dad in Russia for an International Cancer Convention.*

Now it was time to close a door and walk through another. So like my mother, I had to have the same strong resolve at this juncture in my life. I knew that in this situation, I couldn't count on anyone else to necessarily build a new door for me. I would have to design it myself. During the forty-eight hours before the scheduled departure, while I packed and prepared for a five-day, five-country tour, I also prepared my strategy for dealing with the ABC executives, so the move off of *GMA* would go smoothly. Since my morning viewers were loyal, ABC knew they would have a public-relations disaster on their hands if it appeared as though they were firing me. Everyone remembers the negative press that NBC's *Today* show received when Deborah Norville moved into Jane Pauley's seat. As I prepared to leave my seat at *GMA*, I wanted to insure a smooth transition.

STAYING EVEN IS BETTER THAN GETTING EVEN

This was not the first time I had dealt with tumultuous change in my life. Six years ago I went through a painful and public divorce. The divorce process taught me that even in the most stressful situations, staying even is always better than getting even. This means taking a step back and letting go of the emotions of the moment long enough to be able to see which actions will best serve you. Trying to prove yourself right takes a lot of energy. It also takes an emotional toll on you, and it won't necessarily elicit the best outcome. That time you spend drawing a line in the sand could be better used building sand castles.

I've been practicing the philosophy, staying even is better than getting even, for the last four or five years, first with the small stuff, which has prepared me to apply the same principles to the most challenging situations.

Not once have I ever regretted it. Whether it's a breakup, a job change, or a loss of your health or a loved one, you need to learn to change what you can, accept what you can't. Easier said than done? Of course. But I knew I needed to take this to heart, for I needed to stay on an even keel as I navigated the course ahead.

2

Respond, Don't React

The words you speak today

should be soft and tender,

for tomorrow you may have

to eat them.

—Anonymous

Throughout our lives, we face continuous and spontaneous changes. We can't stop them from happening, but we can control how we react to them. One can easily forget about the big picture and simply react to feelings of the moment: revenge, insecurity, or rejection. Rather than reacting emotionally, we need to thoughtfully survey our options and respond intelligently, to set in place a positive future.

Whenever we are confronted with change, we are also being given an opportunity to redefine ourselves, to choose an outcome that will allow us to grow and to be fulfilled. Our first objective is to stay calm and rational. If we respond in this positive way, we can actually influence those around us to act positively, too. Let's remember, conflict cannot survive without our participation.

> *No one can make you feel inferior without your consent.*
>
> —*Eleanor Roosevelt (1884–1962)*

Your ability to respond to confrontation in a calm and rational manner is best achieved when you believe in yourself and are able to set aside your self-doubts. Then you can focus on solutions. Belief in yourself must come *before* accomplishment, not *after*. Using this formula, you will be dealing from strength, not weakness.

DON'T PANIC

For many of us, our initial reaction to change is panic. But remember that panicking and resisting change is nothing more than "hardening of the attitudes."

When panic and resistance set in, it's easy to freeze up and render yourself unable to move, let alone think. It's a vulnerable time and the body's immune system can become compromised. Your blood pressure can shift, you might get headaches or stomachaches, and then the paralysis sets in, both physically and emotionally. For some, a fuzziness also comes, like an incredible heaviness that weighs you down. You may find it difficult to focus, and you're suddenly unable to do the most basic things. Does any of this sound familiar? Some people experience a loss of appetite, while others want to eat everything in sight, attempting to fill up the emptiness by going for instant gratification.

I liken this experience to when your car stalls and you have to restart the engine to get it going again. We must do the same thing with our minds and bodies. Experts tell us that any form of exercise will release stress and clear your mind, so when I needed to get *my* engine restarted, I headed straight to the gym.

Pat Manocchia, fitness expert and director of La Palestra Center for Preventive Medicine, recalls: "The day after Joan had gotten word that they were going to make the change at *GMA*, she came to her workout in what I would call a mild state of shock. There is almost always some level of trauma involved in transition: when you finish high school, when you get married, when you have a baby, when somebody dies, when you move, or when you change jobs. It's all the same. There's the initial disbelief, and then the gradual realization that life is going to change. For each person, that realization manifests differently. Some people sit down and they simply can't move. A kind of paralysis sets in. With others, the opposite happens.

"In Joan's case, I saw that she was moving in the direction of hyperactivity. Her mind was overly active, she was asking herself questions like: What happens now? What do I want to do next? I saw a combination of excitement and anxiety on her face and in her body, and I knew she needed balance. That's the antidote to fear and shock. In the midst of inconsistency, I strive to bring consistency into my clients' lives. Joan needed to know that although so much was changing, she still had something all her own: control over her body and her self-esteem.

"I know that coming to work out that morning helped her adjust more

Me with fitness expert Pat Manocchia.

rapidly to the huge transition that was occurring. Over the years, it's been proven time and again that there are benefits to being physically consistent, just as there are consequences to being physically inconsistent. If you can master your physical being, other things fall into place, because there's a tangible confidence that comes with getting fit.

"Physical exertion also helps to calm the mind. In order to perform, you have to focus, so instead of being scrambled, your mind is forced to take one thing at a time. Joan used her physical activity to give her more breathing room and a wider perspective."

CALL UPON JUDGMENT, NOT EMOTION

A press release about my departure from *GMA* had to be drafted immediately. The ABC executives wanted to announce the change at a convention of the ABC affiliate stations, to be held in Orlando, Florida, in a few weeks. I needed to call upon good judgment and I had to do it quickly.

It's not unusual to have a difficult time thinking clearly and unemotionally when you experience change. You must turn the situation over and over in your mind carefully until you find what will serve you best in the long run, and not simply satisfy your immediate feelings. It's so tempting to blast the other person out of the water. But try imagining the situation as a tornado. In the center of the swirling turbulence is a point of calm. This is your destination, and blasting off will not get you there. Whenever I've been tempted to lash out, I always remember these words of wisdom from one of my grammar-school teachers: *"God gave us two eyes, two ears, and only one mouth. Use them in that ratio."*

Good judgment during my transition meant conveying excitement about my future and gratitude for the two wonderful decades that *GMA* had given me. I wanted my viewers, my morning friends, to embrace my move and follow me wherever I decided to go.

Knowing that my objective should be to remove self-doubt and to keep my focus on the solution, I called my agent and attorney. "Guys, I want to be sure we keep the focus where it belongs," I said. "I'm not interested in addressing the motives of the ABC executives. I'm only interested in addressing my future, and I have nothing but excitement and enthusiasm."

There was silence on the other end of the phone. They knew that although I ultimately had wanted to leave *GMA*, this had to be a huge shake-up in my reality.

STAND LIKE A MOUNTAIN, FLOW LIKE WATER

David Westin, the president of ABC News, would be the one formulating my future role and answering to the press, so I decided I wanted to speak with him myself. Marc, my lawyer, asked me, "Joan, are you sure *you* want to talk to David?"

"I'm sure. I promise you, Marc, I believe I can inspire a positive attitude, even in a network executive."

All I could think about was a book I had read by Brian Luke Seaward, Ph.D., called *Stand Like Mountain, Flow Like Water*. The book's message is that you should stand tall and strong with your convictions and your belief in yourself. At the same time, you should remain flexible and versatile like water, which can change direction at any bend and still manage to reach its destination.

I collected my thoughts as I phoned David Westin. "David," I said, "I've thought a lot about how we can handle this, and basically we have two choices. We can choose the wrong way, which could easily alienate the show's loyal viewers. Or we can take the high road, which will serve us both well.

"I hope we can all remove our egos from this equation, so we can reach a common goal. If our viewers don't feel the network is supporting my move into prime time after all these years, then whoever takes my place could have a very tough time. But if we join hands in this transition, we can avoid all those problems."

There was a brief silence as Westin absorbed my unemotional, practical approach.

I continued, "We *do* need to discuss my role with the network after I leave *GMA*. I'm obviously not leaving ten hours of live programming a week to do one special this next year. If ABC can add four more specials to my contract, then I would have more of a base in prime time. This seems like a good compromise. You know the phrase 'When one door closes, another opens'? Well, I understand that you don't necessarily have any other doors wide open at this exact moment. But giving me some assurances that I'm still going to have a strong presence on ABC will work to serve all of us. In fact, I'll even make appearances on *GMA*."

"You would?" he said, seemingly surprised.

"Yes, of course. I'll be doing prime-time specials on our network. And anyone who does specials on ABC would be an idiot *not* to promote them on *GMA*. So I'll sit next to whoever takes my seat, embrace her, and promote my special. That's called good business for me, and for you, it means I'll be giving my blessing to the new structure of *GMA*."

After even more silence, David agreed; the high road was the only way to proceed to set in place a positive future for all of us. In the days that followed, each time I felt myself filling up with angst, when I got nervous, fearful, or even vengeful, when my muscles tightened, and a knot formed in my stomach, I would use deep breathing to restore my balance. It's not as though I didn't waver. Of course I did. I would catch my inner voice saying, "These guys have allowed the speculation about change on the show to remain unresolved over the last year and have made decisions for which they should be held responsible; they deserve to suffer a little. So why am I letting them off the hook?"

But I knew why. Over the years, this was the way I had chosen to handle my career. I had accepted my job with a smile, even when I knew I might not be getting "my fair share." Back in the seventies, when I first began on *GMA* with David Hartman, he was the star of the show. I was the *other* person. "Don't expect to grow," the executives told me. "You can't be billed as a cohost and you never will, because it's written that way in David's contract." End of discussion.

David had come from a very successful prime-time career and had been cast as the star of the brand-new show *Good Morning America*. The "other" role, never to be called a cohost, was meant to be like an Ed McMahon to Johnny Carson. When I was up for the role, I was required to meet with David's agent before getting the job. His first question to me was, "Would you be willing to change your hair color?"

To this day, I'm not quite sure why he asked that. Was he testing my attitude? My flexibility? Would I do whatever was asked of me? Or did they actually think a brunette would look better alongside David?

"If blond hair doesn't show well on TV," I said evasively, "I'd consider darkening it, but I'd need to better understand the reason for the request."

He moved on. "Do you understand you'll be second banana? And do you have any problem with that?"

*David Hartman—
he showed me the
way on* GMA.

I told him I was well aware of the role and I still thought it was a great opportunity. I passed the test, I got the job, and I didn't have to dye my hair brown. I'll always be grateful to David Hartman for helping me to get the job on *GMA* and for teaching me the ropes. Hardly a day went by that I didn't learn from his advice and his example.

Of course, as society changed and men and women became more equal, my second-banana role seemed out of sync with the times.

I had accepted the role, but the limited job description during that time of exploding women's rights seemed like a kind of dichotomy. Women would write to me and say, "You aren't getting fair billing and it makes us mad just to watch. Why should David Hartman get to interview all the big stars and the diplomats while you get the small stuff? For the sake of women and equality, you should demand to get your equal time and stories."

The early days of GMA.

I could have jumped on that bandwagon and fought for equal time. But that would not have been the best thing for me in the long run. With my eye on the bigger picture, my answer was, "While I understand your frustration, I'm in a position here where I can make a contribution. I happen to have one of the best jobs in television. If I take what they're willing to give me and do my best with that, I'm confident my role will grow."

That was the only way you could really get a fighting chance at advancement during those times. If you fought management, you'd be out of there. That was a given.

Back then, I got the stories on ticks, flower arranging, and fashion faux pas. So how do you stay optimistic? And how do you get noticed ? Early on, Barbara Walters gave me some of the best advice I've ever received, which was not to demand the interviews that my bosses were not yet ready to give women. "You see where fighting City Hall got your predecessors, Joan. Take each spot," she said, "as little as it might be, and make it a gem, make it shine." That advice has served me well in my career and in every aspect of my life.

Can you believe it? Here I was, twenty years later, at the end of my *GMA* career, still following Barbara's advice, making sure that I was shining. The real test of keeping a positive attitude would come when the show left for Scandinavia. I still hadn't told my *GMA* colleagues that I was leaving. This trip was expected to be a tough one, and I didn't want to make it any more difficult. We would be traversing five Scandinavian countries in five days, like the movie *Planes, Trains, and Automobiles*. It was predicted to be cold or rainy almost everywhere. We would have to deal with a new language, a new currency, and a new electrical current on a daily basis. It was tough keeping my secret from the close group with whom I had worked for many years. We had traveled the world together many times over. We were like a family, and I felt that this kind of announcement would be the last straw, since morale was already at an all-time low.

Our crew was used to tough conditions and grueling schedules. So the physical conditions, as bad as they were, were not the only problems. The tension was exacerbated by dealing with the new management. As we arrived in each Scandinavian country, the show's new executives tore apart the preproduced program. Ignoring the fact that this staff had successfully been producing these elaborate trips for years, they disassembled each show, canceling segments that already had been booked and having new guests brought in. Consequently, each morning we would receive a brand-new script in the eleventh hour. It threw the

Barbara Walters with me early on in my career.

entire staff into chaos; all the copy had to be dumped and everybody was up all night long, rebooking and rewriting the show. Needless to say, tempers were short.

By the third day of little to no sleep, we were walking zombies. We had to go on the air each day and make that particular country appear fantastic. We all did our best to stay on an even keel.

My publicity and production manager, Jill Seigerman, who was with us on the trip, remembers: "Joan was on the air a lot less in Scandinavia than usual; I suppose they were phasing her out. As a result, Mindy

On the road with Charlie in Norway and Finland.

Moore, a young newcomer to television, was getting many more segments while Joan was handling less and less. The crew couldn't help but notice. No one understood what was happening. Why was Mindy on the air instead of Joan?

"But Joan just smiled her way through and handled herself beautifully. She was under enormous stress, but she always acted professionally. She was there on time every day, she did her job, she never complained, and nobody on the staff knew what was going on.

"Our last taping of the trip was in Iceland. We gathered before dawn for the broadcast at a site that looked like a gray volcano, in the most miserable weather we had had all week. There was heavy rain and sleet, with winds that were blowing so hard, they blew the rain sideways, right into us. By the time the show was over, we were drenched to the bone; even our underwear was soaked through. With chattering teeth, we climbed onto the bus and collapsed into our seats for the ride to the airport.

"Spencer Christian, our weatherman, had done a segment with a chef that morning, and apparently, there had been a lot of alcohol in his recipe. By the time the chef got on the air, he was tipsy. Somebody sitting on the bus said, 'Hey, Spencer. Your guest looked drunk today.' Spencer laughed.

My right arm, Jill, keeping me on track in Denmark.

Top: *Battling the elements in Iceland.*

Bottom: *Me with GMA staffers—David Goldman, Jill Seigerman, and Tom Touchet.*

"Then one of the ABC executives responsible for many of the last-minute changes that week, piped up. 'Boy,' he said, 'what a week, huh? One of our guests was drunk, another one didn't show up, another one left in the middle to go to the bathroom and didn't get back in time for his spot. I'm surprised nobody got killed.'

"For the first time that entire week, Joan, feeling almost giddy from exhaustion, couldn't let his comment go unanswered. She lifted her head for just a moment and quipped, 'We aren't at the airport yet.' Her comment brought about a roaring round of laughter in the bus."

As soon as we returned to New York, the pressure heated up again. ABC wanted a press release issued immediately, before the affiliates meeting got under way in Florida in just a few days. They sent over a release that ABC had written. I knew I couldn't place my future in the hands of others; the words in this release needed to reflect my heart and my true feelings. I thought about the future, the kind of normal life for which I yearned, and how I wanted a chance to spend more time with my daughters. I sat with Jeff that night and composed a press release that accurately reflected my feelings:

Letting go of GMA *after all these years will not be easy, for I've made many good friends—all of those in front of the camera and behind the camera who have helped make it a winning show over the years, and all the viewers who have faithfully tuned us in each morning. As one door closes, another opens, and I look forward with excitement to my new opportunities.*

After twenty years of waking up America with a smile, and having been given incredible opportunities on Good Morning America, *I will now have a chance to do something I've never done—wake up my own children with a smile, while they're still children.*

May 27, 1997, was a big day. My statement was released to the press. The following day, I made an announcement on the show that I would be leaving in September. A few weeks later, the headline on the *TV Guide* cover read: JOAN ON HER OWN.

It was amazing how much reaction there was to the announcement. But amidst all the hoopla, my work went on as usual. All of the planned appearances and speeches still had to be done. Only now, everywhere I went, every crowd I appeared before looked at me with a new curiosity. How was I dealing with this? Was I happy, sad, excited, frightened? I knew I had a rare opportunity to inspire through my actions at this time. Immediately following the program on which I announced that I was leaving, I set off for the Waldorf-Astoria Hotel to deliver the keynote address to the National Down Syndrome Society. Coincidentally, my pre-planned speech was about the power of positive thinking and making the most of one's life, no matter what it hands you.

For the entire month of May, there was no escaping the effects of this change, since that was all anyone wanted to discuss with me. After a while, I became extremely tired from dealing with other people's emotional reactions and convincing people that I was okay. Every day new requests came for interviews, but I knew that sometimes saying less is better, so I gave no other interviews at that time. June was always a busy month, with school ending and summer plans being made. If ever there was a time to take a long-overdue vacation, it was now. I asked for some time off, knowing the importance of reflecting and regrouping during times of change. I went to Maine to spend some quiet time lying by the lake and walking around the tall pines that surround the summer camp that Jeff owns and operates.

It was an amazing deceleration. I felt like I had just run a marathon. When I finally stopped, I felt like I could barely move. Most of us just don't realize the importance of recovery time. For nearly a week, I found myself so exhausted, I rarely left the cabin and slept the days away. I was actually worried I was sick, but I wasn't. My body just didn't know what to make of it all. I remembered a joke about a young Jewish guy who

TV GUIDE

VIEWER POLL RESULTS
Frank and Kathie Lee Gifford:
Their marriage, their future

EXCLUSIVE
INTERVIEW

"f I never
worked
nother
lay in TV,
t would be
kay. I have
nother life at
ome with
ny daughters."

Joan
On Her
Own

ne 21–27 $1.19

With Jeff, Lindsay, and Sarah at camp in Maine.

grew up with constant heartburn from a diet of pastrami sandwiches and half-sour pickles. He went into the army, and after a week of bland service food, he thought something was drastically wrong with him. He went to the doctor, only to find that there was nothing wrong with his heart; the fire had just gone out in his chest.

In Maine, I vegetated, I meditated, I napped in the middle of the day. I lay on the beach, got some sun, and read incessantly. Whenever I doubted my own strength in creating a positive future, Jeff's unwavering belief in me helped keep me on track. When my friends inadvertently tried to fuel the fire in me with a sense of injustice, Jeff was my calm in the midst of the storm. No matter what, he was always there for me. This retreat took me away from my turbulent environment and allowed me to practice relaxing, a brand-new concept. I was slowing down to the speed of life.

My retreat also took me away from the press. They still wrote articles, they conjectured and predicted, and of course they took to guessing who they thought might take my place—Elizabeth Vargas, Deborah Roberts, Willow Bay, Cynthia McFadden, Connie Chung, or Lisa McRee? Friends, family, and strangers all wanted to know who I thought would be best and how I felt about one of these women filling my shoes. I spent the summer ignoring these questions as best I could. Who was next was not my concern. My new life now filled my thoughts, and I trained my mind to focus on the road ahead.

It's the inner work that you do today, in the moment of stillness and calmness, that gives you the tools to deal with change tomorrow, in the midst of chaos. When I look back, I see that this was all preparation for the grand finale that was approaching: my last show with *Good Morning America*. I spent the summer taking many long weekends in Maine and dabbling in new opportunities. I taped an episode of *Murphy Brown* for CBS and *Lateline* for NBC.

P E O P L E
By MARTHA PICKERILL

DEBORAH FEINGOLD—OUTLINE

Sleeping Late Is the Best Revenge

Who could blame *Good Morning America's* ray of sunshine for feeling burned out after 17 years of morning chat? JOAN LUNDEN announced last week that she will leave the ABC wake-up show in September but will continue to contribute to other ABC News programs. Although rumor had it that she was sidelined because *GMA* has been whipped by NBC's *Today* in the ratings for a year and a half, the network brass said the choice was all hers. At the same time, recollections of Lunden's many interviews —and hairstyles—over the years quickly gave way to speculation about her replacement. The top contenders:

MORNING PERSON	PLUSES	MINUSES
ELIZABETH VARGAS *GMA* news anchor	Experience at all three networks. Besides, she's already sitting there!	Rumors of *All About Eve*–like rivalry with Joan. Can Lunden's fans learn to love her?
DEBORAH ROBERTS *20/20* correspondent, ABC	Worked her way up through NBC's ranks; even got an Emmy nomination for 1992 Olympics coverage.	Wed to Al Roker of NBC's *Today*. No precedent for spouses duking it out in the morning ratings war.
WILLOW BAY *GMA/Sunday* co-anchor	Might attract sports fans (she co-hosts *NBA Inside Stuff*). Oh, and she's married to ABC's president.	Not much industry credibility. She started out as a model, after all, not a newswoman.
CYNTHIA MCFADDEN *Prime Time Live* correspondent, ABC	A résumé chock-full of heavy-hitting, award-winning, serious-journalist stuff.	Can't quite see her whipping up an egg-white omelette with Richard Simmons.
CONNIE CHUNG Former *CBS Evening News* co-anchor	She's available (DreamWorks just canned her talk show with husband Maury Povich)—and likable.	That thing with Newt Gingrich's mom.

ABC (4)-PACE—SYGMA

Lily Tomlin,
Candace Bergen,
and me, taping
Murphy Brown

Each of these new experiences opened my eyes and my mind to the prospect of doing something different. And of course, I had Jeff, who offered constant comfort and support. I'll never forget his words of advice that summer in Maine:

A Bend in the Road
Is Not the End of the Road,
If You Remember to Take the Turn.

RIGHT: *Whatever is around the bend, I've got to get ready for it!*

3

Take the High Road

When you start down the road
to revenge, remember to dig
two graves.

—Chinese proverb

When you were a very small child, I'll bet you were taught the Golden Rule: Do unto others as you would have them do unto you.

When you were older, it evolved into: What goes around, comes around.

Both expressions said the same thing: Treat others as you would like to be treated.

The lesson I most remember learning from my mom is: If you don't have something nice to say, don't say anything at all. Or another one of her favorites, which works every time: If you want to get back at someone, kill 'em with kindness. Be bigger than they are. It was actually Oscar Wilde who first said, "Always forgive your enemies. Nothing annoys them so much."

We carry these simple but profound lessons with us all through life. In times of distress, we can call upon these tenets to find the grace within to deal with the changes without.

FIND THE GRACE WITHIN TO DEAL WITH THE CHANGES WITHOUT

The power to choose a higher path is yours. Your thoughts within affect the direction you take. Grace, dignity, and self-confidence lead you to that higher road. These are qualities that each and every one of us can learn and develop with each new accomplishment in our lives.

Acting with grace and dignity means coping with difficult situations with your head held high. It means appearing comfortable at the most uncomfortable times. It means understanding when to speak up and when to listen. It's going through life acting as if the person you love most is looking over your shoulder. The picture we present on the outside says a lot about what's going on inside. Finding your grace and dignity will often help others to find theirs.

These philosophies have served me not only in times of crisis but also in the simplest of situations. I'm sure you've all had an encounter with a coworker, a boss, a partner, or a friend when you could have used my mom's words echoing in your ears: Be bigger than they are. Kill 'em with kindness.

There is more to knowing than just being correct.

—*Benjamin Huff*

I recall a particular producer I worked with on *Good Morning America* who, I believe, didn't have a high opinion of women. The first few times he came into the makeup room to talk to me before the show, he clearly projected a negative attitude that said, "I have more important things to do."

I must admit that I took a certain degree of pleasure and amusement in sending the same negative energy back to him. It was very unlike me, but I initially thought it was warranted because he didn't even try to mask his opinion that women were not very high on the food chain.

Then I took a step back and said to myself: "Don't I have a knot in my stomach after this kind of encounter? And I'm about to walk downstairs to say, 'Good morning, America!' I'm supposed to brighten people's day and start them off right. Reacting to this man with negativity is antithetical, not at all productive, and it's getting in the way of my work and my positive attitude. How long can we keep doing this?" Indira Gandhi said: "You cannot shake hands with a clenched fist."

I reached into my bag of tricks and remembered my mother's words. To kill 'em with kindness meant ignoring his negativity and feeding him positive energy instead. The next time this producer came to see me before the show, I was smiling and enthusiastic. I asked him his opinion about my upcoming interviews. As I engaged him in conversation, I did not react to anything he said or did that was less than respectful. Very quickly, the antagonism melted away and we both felt better. My mornings became more peaceful and positive. It's not important whether or not I changed his opinion of women—it was important for me to safeguard my morning preparation time for the program. I had followed a tenet I learned years ago: don't choose to be right, choose to be happy. In this situation, taking the higher road allowed the two of us to find a way to work together amicably and productively.

You can apply these same principles in your life. When you take the time to understand the inner workings of your relationships and the reactions of other people, you start to develop the tools that help you find the grace within. It begins with the ability to step back, take a breath, and acknowledge your emotions and how they might be coloring your thoughts and your reactions. Then consider the emotions that others might be feeling and that might be guiding *their* reactions. With all this objective observation, you can think about what you want to say and do next.

> *There is no loss in letting the branches bend, when resisting the wind would cause them to break.*
>
> — *The Buddha*

Remember that each thought, each response, will guide you along your life's path. Ask yourself: Will I be able to live with my response tomorrow? Next week? Next year? Is this the best thing for me in the long run? Will it lead me to my desired destination?

SURVEY YOUR OPTIONS

As you drive down a highway, you can't stare at the pavement in front of you or you'll crash. You need to look ahead to where you're going and at all of your options. Only then can you safely navigate the twists and turns before you.

The same holds true in navigating our lives. It's important to avoid the smaller myopic moments and look at the big picture. The key is not drawing that little line in the sand and proving yourself right at each juncture. It's letting go of initial reactions and viewing whatever occurs at each bend as an opportunity filled with challenge, excitement, intrigue, and promise.

You won't learn this in the middle of a crisis. You'll learn it by practicing these skills in low-stress situations when the stakes are not so high. You must practice in times of calmness, so that you'll have the tools you'll need in times of crisis. This means keeping your eyes open as you travel your path, so change doesn't always have to take you by surprise.

Every now and then, we all get sideswiped by a crisis. But more often than not, there were signposts. We knew what was coming. We saw yellow lights or even red flags along the way, but ignored them because we didn't want to face the situation. Of course, it never went away.

The truth is that we have no control over many of the events of our lives. While thinking and planning ahead frequently soften the blow, change can still feel like you're being hit by a freight train, even when you know it's coming down the track. It's hard to make decisions when you're being dragged underneath that fast-moving train, banging against the ground. But if you can learn to look at a situation like an uninvolved third person without emotional attachment, you can free yourself of the illusion that change is battering you. Free of that attachment, you can calmly assess your options with perspective, grace, and courage. You can choose the options that work best for you.

BE YOUR OWN SPIN DOCTOR

Sometimes, if we can alter our thinking a little bit, we can completely change a situation. Someone once told me that you can't rewrite yesterday's news, but you can influence what you read tomorrow morning. Think about the outcome you would like to achieve. Now adjust your

> *The good news is, that the bad news can be turned into good news when you change your attitude.*
>
> —*Robert Schuller*

thinking to accommodate that. I liken the process of choosing the outcome that will serve you best to the practice used by so many politicians and large corporations.

I'm sure you've all heard the term *spin doctor*. Corporations pay people small fortunes for the sole purpose of "spinning" a potentially bad situation into a good one. If a company is downsizing, moving to another city, or even coming out with a new product, they want to be sure to put the best face on it. It's all about presentation, focusing on the positive aspects of a situation. Politicians learn early on that facing people with a positive attitude has a direct impact on the way people respond to them and whatever is happening. You can learn to be your own spin doctor inside your own head.

As I looked forward to September 5, my farewell broadcast on *Good Morning America*, putting a positive spin on my attitude toward my last show was my personal goal and my challenge. Everywhere I went, I was constantly asked, "How are you going to feel? Aren't you going to be sad?" Actually, no. What could be better or more fulfilling than a celebration of a person's accomplishments? A few veteran producers were assigned to produce a "tribute" show for the final morning. They wanted the whole thing to be a wonderful surprise. I didn't know exactly what was being planned, but I was ready to appreciate and enjoy it.

Jill Seigerman helped produce the final show:

"As we were preparing for Joan to leave the show, things were crazier than ever. While we were moving out of our offices and dressing room, we were also trying to put a wonderful show together. Secretly, I was meeting with Randy Barone, Eric Beesemyer, and Patty Neger, longtime producers from *GMA* who were very close to Joan. Our goal was to best highlight the breadth of her twenty-year career. Not a small task. For every decision we made, we took into consideration how she would feel and react. We sorted through four thousand broadcasts that spanned two decades to find Joan's best interviews, her most memorable moments, her parade of hairstyles, and the wackiest fiascoes. And we had to keep it all from Joan, which was hard because she is so hands-on in her career.

"Every person we contacted, from President Clinton to President Bush, Chevy Chase to Tim Allen, and Celine Dion to Michael Bolton, wanted to be involved in the program and honor Joan."

For the first time, I was going to walk onto the set with no script, no list of guests, and no knowledge of what was about to happen. I always liked to be well prepared and in control. But for this show, the only control I would have would be the spin I put on the experience. I wanted this show to be exciting, uplifting, and fun. I knew that my participation and the way I presented myself on the air would have an impact on how I flowed into the next phase of my life.

So how would I do it? Would I allow myself to be consumed with fearful thoughts like, "Oh my God, this life as I know it ends today"? Or would I choose to greet America with the inner strength and excitement that told them something great was happening? It was clearly my choice. I knew that a change this paramount was disconcerting, but I also knew I was satisfied, even satiated, with my *GMA* career. I was ready to move into new territory. How hard could it be?

I remember, years ago, interviewing an expert on trauma and grief counseling, who said that it took three to five years for a person to get over a major life change like divorce or loss of a loved one, and be ready to rejoin life. I also remember thinking that he was crazy. I had been recently divorced at the time and I didn't want to believe that it could take that long before I'd pick up the pieces and move on. I thought, "Three months, maybe six, I'll be back to normal." But years passed and

A BEND IN THE ROAD IS NOT THE END OF THE ROAD

it turned out that the expert was right. Most people who've been through a major life change will agree that it *does* take a long time. It was, in fact, three years before I felt ready to rejoin the dating game and look toward a new life. After seeing how long it took to restart my life then, here I was facing a whole new way of life again.

That question "What's going to happen next?" can bring excitement and anxiety. It's the question on which soap operas are based, although we do like our own lives to be a little less melodramatic. But uncertainty can make us afraid of what might be around the bend, and that's when our imaginations go to work. My mind conjured up a picture of myself, lying around aimlessly, not knowing what to do. I would gain fifty pounds by eating tortilla chips and watching the soaps all day long. Of course, that image couldn't be further from the way my life is now. However, for a short time, I did allow my mind to wander down that path toward the fear of change, the fear of the unknown.

Good futures are not created by fear. Instead, you can put your mind and your imagination to work for you, creating dreams and goals. You can allow yourself to be paralyzed by fear, or you can ask questions just as easily, like: Am I destined to compose a song? Write a book? Produce a movie? Own my own business? Who knows what the future holds? A Nobel Prize? A seat in Congress? An Academy Award?

Each of us has innate talents and abilities, and our task in the face of change is to believe in ourselves and the brightness of our future. Then everything becomes clearer and it's as if right decisions are made *for* us. I'm reminded of a proverb:

Only when you stop, look back at

> *If you let cloudy water settle, it will become clear.*
> *If you let your upset mind settle, your course will also become clear.*
>
> — *The Buddha*

52

your accomplishments, and become aware of your assets and talents can you better see where you're going. Sometimes the extraordinary things can seem very ordinary, because they are a part of our everyday life.

Jeff recalls: "Joan didn't usually take the time to appreciate her accomplishments. She was always so busy doing what she does, I think she lost perspective. But the truth is, she had traveled around the entire world, she had interviewed every powerful politician, world leader, and anybody else who was making the news. And she just did it because it was her job. She hardly thought about it; it became second nature.

"I reminded her to think about the opportunities she'd had. I knew that if she had an appreciation for all that she had accomplished, then she'd be more receptive to embracing the change. Because Joan is a celebrity, people naturally expected her to land on her feet no matter what. But Joan is a human being, as vulnerable as the next person. When it was time to leave her former identity and face the unknown, I wanted to be the net underneath the tightrope. But on a lot of levels, Joan is such a strong individual, although she knew the net was there, she never lost her balance."

I felt like I was being tested daily. The press never gave up trying to corner me. I was even approached by strangers in the street to see if I was really as okay as I purported to be. Whether it was on TV talk shows, in magazines and newspapers, or on satellite radio, every interviewer asked the same questions: "How are you going to deal with that last day? Are you going to cry? Won't it be emotional for you? After all, this isn't just a job change, it's a change of your national identity."

I looked at each press interview as a job in itself, choosing an interesting and different approach, depending on which interviewer I would be facing. For the David Letterman show, always an unpredictable experience, I called the producers ahead of time. "There's nothing that I won't answer," I told them, "but there's something I want to do. I want to smash my alarm clock on the air." They loved the idea. I brought the clock and they provided the sledgehammer and protective glasses. By thinking it through and making this suggestion, I was able to put a humorous and positive spin on the interview. By the way, I have yet to replace that alarm clock.

As difficult as some of those interviews were, they made me stop and think more deeply about how I wanted to approach the last show. I had completed my work, it was a job well done, and I didn't want to be whiny. I didn't want to look like a blithering idiot and sob my way through the show. I wanted to leave with grace.

It's hard to look at a new door with wonder when you haven't passed through it yet. But my last several months at *GMA* really were wonderful. It wasn't like stepping into the same job every day; the sameness was gone. I approached each show as an audition for whatever I would be doing next, and there was a new kind of freedom. I believe that the mind is like a computer and whatever we input, that's what we'll think and do. I worked hard at inputting my computer, thinking about each interview, literally laying out my plans for the months before my departure. I walked downstairs each day to do the show, viewing it as an opportunity to go out there and be the best I had ever been. I was shaping my own destiny.

The morning of September 5, when I awakened before dawn, I realized it was the first time in seventeen years that I didn't have an eighty-page script to read. I stepped into the shower with a mission; I was about to program the morning with the spin that I wanted it to have. I knew it was up to me to set the tone, that if I broke down and cried, others could take their cues from me. I stood in the shower and repeated over and over: "Today is a celebration. Today is a celebration."

As the splash of hot water hit my body, I remembered twenty years ago, starting out in New York as a reporter. I had been quite naive and

Smashing my alarm clock on The Late Show with David Letterman.

everybody had taken their potshots at me because I was "the new blonde in town," trying to get ahead in the very male business of news reporting. The first time I was asked to anchor the six o'clock news, it didn't elicit a good response from WABC-TV *Eyewitness News* anchor Roger Grimsby. He was a veteran who had come up through the ranks of newspaper and radio, and when they told him that I would be sharing his anchor desk so early on in my career, he was furious. A rather gritty, salty, tough character, he threw his script on the floor and said, "She doesn't deserve to anchor. She hasn't been to the school of hard knocks. She hasn't paid her dues, the price to sit at the anchor desk."

Joan Lunden WABC-TV Eyewitness News

As a reporter on Eyewitness News *in 1976.*

I was insulted at the time, but he was right. I had just come from the little homogenized town of Sacramento, where I cleaned weather maps, got the coffee, and eventually graduated from doing the weather to anchoring local news. Getting out on the streets was another world and a necessary part of the process of learning about hard-core reality. I needed those years as a street reporter, feeling the pain of people losing their homes to fire, experiencing the angst of families confronted by violence, getting a taste of the frailties and tragedies of life. I needed to build layers of empathy and compassion for others. I'm grateful for the five years I spent as a reporter on the streets of New York. I needed to understand the problems of the world in order to be the host of a national program like *GMA*, where I'd have to ad-lib about crises as they arose.

I did anchor the news that week with Roger. Coincidentally, it was the same week that Barbara Walters moved from the *Today* show to the *ABC Evening News* with Harry Reasoner. Harry wasn't happy about sharing his news desk with Barbara, either. He wouldn't even speak to her when they got into the same elevator at the ABC studio. This idea that the women were moving into the men's domain was not popular at all. There had been published reports that Sam Donaldson got on the speaker system in the ABC newsroom and called out, "The women are coming! The women are coming!" As I sat there with Roger at the anchor desk, each time he would end a story and throw it to me, he called me Barbara instead of my name. I guess he thought it was symbolic of the female onslaught of the week.

In retrospect, I can't really blame Roger, Harry, or Sam. They were just resisting change, a very natural human reaction. For me, it was an experience that would teach me to face adversity, believe in myself and my capabilities, and remain calm while rising to the occasion.

Working on a news show is kind of like being in the eye of a hurricane. The job of the host is not just about reading copy; it's about getting inside of people's heads and hearts. If you don't have those layers of empathy and compassion, it shows. I would also come to learn that being at the top means being willing to take up the slack for anyone or anything that needed to be done to get the show on the air. It's not about being on a pedestal; it's about having the attitude that nothing is beneath you.

Many years ago, Barbara Walters hosted the *Today* show with Dave Garroway. Back then it was Barbara's job to do live commercials on the show. One morning, just before an Alpo dog food commercial, Barbara stood behind a table with a big golden retriever. The clock was ticking for the commercial to begin, fifteen seconds, ten seconds, at which point the dog pooped right on the table. The crew looked on, horrified, staring at the fresh pile of doggie-doo. "Five seconds," said a nervous stage manager. The show's executive producer, Stuart Schulberg, happened to be standing nearby. When no one else moved, Stu took a quick step forward.

Four seconds—he put his hand at the side of the table.

Three seconds—he scooped the entire pile off the table into his other hand.

Two seconds—he stepped away.

One second—Barbara said, "I'm here today with Rusty, our Alpo friend. He loves his Alpo."

As the dog rushed to the bowl to gobble up the Alpo, Stuart stood by the side, his hands full. Thirty seconds later, it was all over. A tape machine rolled the next commercial. Stuart looked at the crew and the college interns who had stood there motionless, watching him. He held his hand out and said, "This is the difference between what you do and what I do." He had saved the commercial by doing whatever it took to get the job done.

As I stood in the shower, I continued to think back to my first few days as a reporter out on the streets of New York City. It had all seemed quite overwhelming. For my very first story, I was sent to the New York State Supreme Court to cover a bombing-and-conspiracy trial. Besides the tiny courthouse in Fair Oaks, California, where I had fought a traffic ticket (I won), I had never been inside a real courtroom before. We pulled up in front of the impressive Greek Revival building with huge columns and a long, wide staircase leading up to its massive doors. Herb Todd, the cameraman on this assignment, said, "This is it. Let's do it!" He got out of the car into the maelstrom of camera crews and reporters. Herb opened the trunk and asked quite matter-of-factly, "How many magazines do you want?"

"Oh, thanks," I answered, "but I think I'm going to be much too busy in the courtroom to be reading magazines."

He looked at me in disbelief. You see, magazines are the canisters that were used to hold the film for a TV camera before the advent of videotape. After the crew managed to catch their breath from hysterical laughter, Herb said, "Okay, so we have a lot to teach you. This is a camera, Joan." He held it up for me to see. "And this is a magazine. The film goes inside the magazine and you can have seven hundred feet of film or fifteen hundred, depending on how many interviews you think you're going to do. Or how long the story is going to be. I'll just grab a couple of seven hundreds. Okay?"

I nodded and walked toward the courthouse. I headed to the courtroom where the trial was taking place, and my next task was to find the other reporters, so I would know where to sit. Herb yelled at me through the noise, "Hey, Joan, we can't go in. Only reporters allowed. When it's over, if the defendant is found innocent, she'll be coming out, so stick by her right hip. We'll find you as soon as you get outside. If she's guilty she won't be coming out at all, so stick like glue to her attorney."

I wondered how in the world I would ever be able to find my crew amidst so much chaos. Once inside, I took a seat beside several men with notebooks (I figured those would be the reporters). When the session ended, the defendant was found guilty, so as Herb had instructed, I found her attorney and stuck to him like glue. To my amazement, when the courtroom doors opened and everyone poured out onto the steps, there were Herb and the crew, lights on, camera rolling. The crew had found me and we left with a story—a true miracle, as far as I was concerned.

The next day, I was sent out on a fire, a massive blaze in an abandoned warehouse somewhere along the Hudson River. As we pulled up in front, the flames were shooting out of the windows and there was smoke everywhere. At least twenty fire trucks were on the scene and scores of firemen were running all over the place. It was chaotic and I didn't know with whom to talk in order to get the details for my story. As the film crew took their shots, I stopped a fireman to ask a few questions. Needless to say, he didn't stop to answer me.

I would later learn that you're only supposed to get your reports from the man in the white hat, the chief. Not from the guys in the black hats, who are too busy fighting the fire to answer. Okay, so this was the learning curve. I had to remember that I'd never been to a fire *or* the Supreme Court.

My move to New York didn't just teach me about television. It taught me about life. When I arrived in the Big Apple from Sacramento, where everyone drives their cars everywhere they go, believe it or not, I had never taken public transportation. A friend who had moved to New York several years before had helped me find a temporary apartment at Sixty-third Street and Park Avenue on the East Side of Manhattan. A very chic area, but of course, the whole one-bedroom apartment was the size of the living room in my Sacramento condo and cost me a whopping $750.00 a month. Each day, I took a taxi across town to the *Eyewitness News* studio on the West Side and then back home again. A few dollars over and a few dollars back. Definitely above my budget. One day, when another reporter saw me getting out of a taxi, he said, "You're gonna eat up everything you make if you take taxis everywhere. All you have to do is walk two blocks up from your apartment and take a crosstown bus."

"Okay, thanks," I said. The next morning, I walked the two blocks, found the bus stop, and waited. The bus pulled up, the back doors opened before me, I got in, and as the bus pulled away I found a seat. I noticed people staring at me. "Wow," I thought, "I've only been on the air for ten days and it's amazing how many people are already recognizing me." They continued to stare, and when the bus pulled up to the corner where the ABC building was located, I got off. "Well," I thought, "that wasn't so bad." That weekend, I found a more reasonable apartment right across the street from the newsroom and moved, so I was able to walk to work.

About three months later, a snowstorm shut down New York City, and I was sent out with a crew to cover the story. It was the same crew and cameraman from the conspiracy trial and the fire. We had to travel across town and all the way out to Brooklyn. Since the city had been brought to a halt, subways and buses were the only feasible mode of transportation. We got on the subway and when we emerged from the subway station, we still had to take a bus to get to our destination in Brooklyn. When the bus pulled up, the crew went to get on, walking to the front of the bus and entering by the front door. We stepped on, passing that little machine where you were supposed to toss in your fare. The cameraman said, "Go on, Joan, I got you, don't worry," as he dropped some money into the fare box.

I walked to the back, took a seat, and I began to laugh so hard, tears came to my eyes. People hadn't been staring at me three months ago because I was famous. They were staring at me because I was *infamous*. I had gotten on the back of the bus and hadn't paid the fare. Having never before taken public transportation, it hadn't occurred to me. I told my crew between bursts of laughter and they also laughed until they cried.

My last reflection was about my very first day as cohost on *Good Morning America*. For two years, I had filled in for the previous cohosts, Nancy Dussault and Sandy Hill, while I was still working at *Eyewitness News*. The day I got the call from ABC that I had the *GMA* job, I also got the call that I was pregnant with my first child. After a brief maternity leave, the day finally came to assume my new role. It was a time of overwhelming change—a new job and a new baby. Jamie was just eight weeks old and I was planning to take her to work with me. For ABC, this was a new concept in business. As for me, I had never even changed a diaper before, so I was learning as I went along. I lifted Jamie from her bassinet at four in the morning, bundled her up, and got into the ABC car that was to take us to the studio. Naturally, I was very nervous, and to add to the chaos of that first morning, the car broke down on the highway on our way into town. We got out, and thank God, some nice man who was driving by stopped and took us to a taxi stand nearby. We went the rest of the way into the city by taxi with me nursing Jamie and trying to read my script. Talk about unnerving!

I also remember the first time Barbara Walters sat in for vacationing David Hartman. Even though she had worked this early schedule for years on the *Today* show, I noticed she had a hard time wiping the "sleepy" out of her eyes when she arrived at the studio at 5:30 A.M. But what really opened her eyes that morning was the sight of infant Jamie nestled into her crib in my dressing room. As I entered the room, Barbara was standing over the crib in total disbelief. She looked at me and said, "I can't even imagine what my bosses back at the *Today* show would have

Introducing baby Jamie on my first day as host of GMA.

said if I had tried to bring my daughter in to work with me when she was an infant. Boy, have times changed!"

So now, here I was, twenty years later. I turned off the water and stepped out of the shower filled with gratefulness, so proud and happy to have gotten where I was. But I had an odd feeling. Over the years I had developed an uncanny sense of knowing exactly when my driver arrived. I even sensed when a substitute driver had taken his place. That last

With Barbara Walters and my daughters in April 1997.

morning, somehow I knew he wasn't there. When I looked in the drive-
way, sure enough, there was no car at all.

I called the car company, only to find that in all the madness of the last
show, a mistake had been made on the pickup sheet. They said, "We got
a message that you were staying overnight in the city and we have you
scheduled for a five o'clock pickup there. We could send a car, but it'll
never arrive in time."

"Don't worry. I'll drive in myself." I hung up the phone and smiled.
Life had such an odd way of repeating itself. My time with *Good Morning*

America began without a ride to the studio and it was ending the same way. Only this time the car didn't break down; it never arrived at all! So on my last day of work, I drove myself into New York City to the studio, laughing all the way. Funny how things come full circle.

Jill Seigerman recalls: "I was already at the studio when I heard that the car hadn't been sent. Even though it hadn't bothered Joan at all, I was devastated. I wanted her to be as relaxed as possible, because not only was it her very last show, it was also the first time she would ever go on *GMA* to do two hours of live television without a script. We had a ton of surprises planned and Joan had trusted us enough not to ask any questions.

"On top of that, the dressing room that Joan had occupied for so many years was in chaos. ABC had given her no leeway at all; we had to have Joan's things out of the dressing room and the office by the end of the day so they could redo both of them for Lisa McRee. There were boxes filled with Joan's wardrobe stacked everywhere and the walls were already bare. Just being there was an emotional experience, and I wanted Joan to walk on the set with her mind as clear as possible. I was concerned that Joan would be affected by everyone else's emotions. Many members of the staff and crew felt like they had grown up with her and they were quite emotional.

"Joan got a little teary-eyed when she walked on the set to a standing ovation. Normally, she's in a dark studio in the morning with just the cameramen—it's a closed set with no audience. But that morning, the studio was brimming with over one hundred people: family, friends, producers from the past, executives."

I was feeling great, but my colleagues, albeit with the best of intentions, weren't making it any easier for me to keep my composure. On my way downstairs to the set, they kept running up to me, saying: "I just wanted to say good-bye before the show started." They'd give me a kiss and burst into tears. I felt the swell of their emotions but I had prepared myself so well during the five or six weeks prior to the show, nothing could shake me.

When I took my seat at seven o'clock, there was an air of mystery and excitement. There was an outpouring of love from my children, my mother, Jeff, and my friends. And then there were all the people I had worked with over the years, my other family with whom I had spent almost as much time as I had with my real family: stage directors, camera operators, the TelePrompTer operator, lighting and audio crew, stage-hands, and all of the people who had been with me since Day One. They had lived through my three pregnancies and the accompanying morning sickness, they had watched me gain and lose fifty pounds, and many of them had held, fed, burped, and changed my daughters. Also there were my agents, my lawyer, my publicist, the producers of my prime-time specials, my fitness trainers, my book agent, and my book publishers. My entire support team was there, giving the morning an energy all its own.

And of course, there was Charlie Gibson, my cohost for ten years, the man whom I had sat beside each morning, no matter what was going on in my life. There had been mornings when he would just look at me and finish my sentence. Charlie is a very sentimental guy, and Jill was afraid he would break down. When I took my seat that morning, he was almost afraid to look at me.

The show started with a bang. I was floored when the *GMA* logo and theme music were followed by a videotaped greeting from President Clinton, saying: "Good morning, Joan. Hillary and I want to tell you how much we'll miss you in the morning. You really became, some days, the company misery loves, for no matter how early we had to wake up, we always knew that you had already been up for hours.

"For nearly twenty years, you've been a wonderful part of our mornings, keeping us informed about the issues that matter the most to American families, amazing us with your daredevil stunts, and always pre-

No matter what was going on, Charlie and I could always make each other laugh.

senting the news of the day in a positive light. America's mornings won't be the same without you, but we look forward to watching you in prime time. Thanks for twenty great years on *GMA* and enjoy the extra sleep."

The Bushes and the Fords also wished me well on videotape, as did Michael Douglas, George Clooney, John Travolta and Kelly Preston, Michael Bolton, Billy Joel, Bruce Willis and Demi Moore, Danny DeVito, Tim Allen, and Richard Lewis. The first live guests of the morning were a couple of my news anchor cohorts, Paula Zahn and Diane Sawyer, who talked about their stints on morning television and how tough it was.

They introduced a video hello from Barbara Walters (from London, covering Princess Diana's death) who had been such a mentor over the years. She offered me a warm farewell and a hope that I would finally get some rest. Remember, Barbara had also made this same transition from early-morning television—the *Today* show—and had told me on a number of occasions how difficult an adjustment it had been.

In an effort to help incoming host Lisa McRee with her adjustment, I presented her with a "dawn patrol" basket. Among other things, it included an alarm clock, No-Doz, and an eye mask and ear plugs so she could catch up on sleep during the day. When I first heard that Lisa got the job, I had spent some time on the phone with her, sharing the ins and outs of maneuvering a live morning program like *GMA*.

Diane Sawyer and Paula Zahn join me on my final GMA show.

The producers shuffled me out from time to time and brought in the stars they had kept hidden in private rooms in the studio. The cast of various television shows sent video farewells and the cast of *Rent* was there in person to perform their hit song "Seasons of Love."

Nostalgic clips were shown of my long history on the air, including presidential inaugurations; royal weddings; exhilarating adventures like scaling glaciers in Alaska, bungee jumping in New Zealand, and flying in an F-16 jet with the Thunderbirds; and a hysterical historical perspective of my hairdos over the years.

While the show went on inside the studio, Spencer Christian, *GMA*'s weatherman, took his typical good humor out on the street, and talked to fans who had come to watch. The next wonderful surprise was Chevy Chase, who appeared at our news desk for a very funny "look back" at my career. I had always loved his hilarious rendition of the news on *Saturday Night Live*.

Cast of Rent *performing on my tribute show.*

TOP: *Chevy Chase delivering a "Lunden retrospective" at the* GMA *news desk.*

BOTTOM: *Me with Chevy.*

Who ever gets a gift like this? I sat back and enjoyed every minute of it and I held myself together—until Celine Dion appeared. She was a huge surprise. As the producers were preparing the show, they had asked me which performers I wanted to have there. I put Celine's name on the top of the list. I was told that while Celine wanted to be there for my last show, she was in a studio making an album, so she wouldn't be able to make the appearance.

I held it together until they surprised me with Celine Dion.

Celine and I go back a long way. I was one of the first people to interview her as she started her singing career in the United States, with the title song for *Beauty and the Beast*. French being her native language, she had still been struggling with her English and was uneasy about her ability to put a complete sentence together. I assured her that together, we would make it a great interview. I offered her strength and friendship. Over the years, whenever she came out with a new album, she would

Me and Celine.

always come to our show first and ask for me. We shared a mutual respect and admiration. Several years later, I had the chance to go on the road with her concert tour for one of my *Behind Closed Doors* specials. She took me out onstage with her in front of a tremendous crowd, which made me nervous. Now it was her turn to give *me* strength.

When she walked on the set of my tribute show and began to sing, "You were my strength when I was weak. You were my voice when I couldn't speak," I was filled with emotion. I knew what that song meant to her, how much she loved her husband, René, and that she sang it to him. My eyes found Jeff, who had been all of those things to me throughout this tumultuous time.

At the last show with Jeff, who was by my side every step of the way.

72

You gave me wings and made me fly.
You touched my hand. I could touch the sky.
I lost my faith, you gave it back to me.
You said no star was out of reach.

Okay, this was a tearjerker. Jeff and Jill were like angels for me throughout the taping, sticking close by and watching over me. I appreciated it, but I was well prepared and I enjoyed the celebration as much as everyone else did. I could have gotten bogged down, worrying about my future and grieving over what I would be missing, but that's not the way I felt. So I sat back, ready to appreciate my past and revel in the possibilities of my future.

I ended the show with a statement that I had prepared:

I really want to say thank you to a number of people. I want to say thank you, of course, to all my colleagues, those who work behind the cameras, behind the desks, who helped put this broadcast together in order for us to be out here. Of course, my support team. Charlie, I promise I'll call, I'll write. I know you'll call me early in the morning, I know you will. I also want to thank Spencer, who gave me so many good jokes, and David Hartman, who showed me the ropes. I also want to thank my daughters, Jamie, Lindsay, and Sarah, for putting up with the demands of this crazy job, my schedule, and my sleep deprivation. I will be there now to wake you up in the mornings.

I thank the people who have given me support. First of all, my original guru, my mother, who always said I could do anything I wanted to do. A heartfelt thanks to my constant Rock of Gibraltar, Jeff, the love of my life. And, of course, to you the viewers. And I don't know if you realize this, but I feel I've had a very close relationship with all of you, even though you haven't been able to speak to me.

I thank you very much. This has been a rare and privileged seat from which to view the world and be where history is being made. And it's more than anyone could ever hope for in a lifetime.

Thank you all.

My mom, Gladyce, Jamie, Lindsay, Jeff, and Sarah with me at the teary finale.

I had taken the high road, which gave me a good sense of direction as I was about to round this next bend. It was time to go home, sleep past dawn, and be there for my girls, Jeff, and the rest of my life. My future was waiting.

RIGHT: *There's no looking back now.*

4

To Predict the Future, Create It

To each of us, at certain points
of our lives, there come
opportunities to rearrange our
formulas and assumptions—not
necessarily to be rid of the old,
but more to profit from adding
something new.

—Leo Buscaglia

As I began creating my future, I found a card that I sent to some of my friends to let them know I was ready to embark on this new journey. It said:

The only way to find out what's on the other side is to walk through the door.

As I walked through the door into this brand-new life, I knew little about my future. I only knew it would be different—very different. Before I could begin molding a master business plan, I needed to start with the basics, and I do mean the basics: When was I going to wake up in the mornings? Without the demanding structure of the early-morning show, did I need to put myself on an arbitrary schedule? Did I still need to go to bed early? In the first few weeks I found myself staying up with my daughters until they actually had to say, "Mom, it's midnight. We have school tomorrow." I almost wanted the people around me to give me a bedtime because the freedom was overwhelming.

Sarah, Jamie, and Lindsay monkey around the GMA set.

I was uneasy with the loss of a framework in my life. I felt like there was no reason to go to my office, even though it would take months just to answer the thousands of letters that had come in during my final days at *GMA*. Many of these letters helped me acknowledge my achievements and gain some perspective on the transition—from presidents to all those who had helped me during my years at *GMA* to the many viewers who simply wrote to say good-bye. Then there were the offers coming in— talk shows, sitcoms, movies. Why do we always doubt that we will receive them when others are so sure? Why is it that so many others could have the vision to see me doing so many things in this new phase of my life? This obviously was a life lesson.

VISUALIZE YOUR FUTURE

Why is it that we seem to define ourselves and what we can do with our lives only by what we are currently doing, or by what we've done in the past? Shouldn't we expand that vision to include all the things at which we might be good, if we just had the courage to try? By increasing our options, we increase the power we have over our future. We should never limit the number of doors through which we can walk. We must be able to visualize that future in order to achieve it.

As I began to settle into my new life, I found it difficult to visualize *my* future. With the uneasiness that came with uncertainty, I began accepting engagements as insurance against the unknown. I booked speeches, I took lunches, I listened to pitches, and I scheduled early-morning workouts. I created a massive "to do" list, just to fill in time—time that I didn't really have.

> *Life is a great big canvas and you should throw all the paint on it you can.*
>
> *—Danny Kaye*

I have seen so many people create their own impossible "to do" lists that they'll never be able to achieve. They end up living their lives like one big emergency, frantically trying to keep up and live up to expectations that they themselves have imposed. Then, when they can't pull it off, they feel like failures.

What a setup! If people would take a realistic look at the list of things they think they should do each day, they would have to acknowledge the fact that it's often impossible. There's too much on the list and too little time for themselves, unless they want to be frenzied all day long and worn out. When you work out your body, everyone knows that you need to stop in between exercises—take time to breathe, lower your heart rate, and reenergize. The same holds true for our day-to-day lives. We all need to stop and take some time to catch our breath and think about things, so we can face our challenges with a calmer and clearer outlook. Without stepping back to renew, we can lose track of ourselves and our goals, moving through life in a constant state of frustration and exhaustion.

Many of my friends felt that I had been on a high-speed carousel for so long, I would never be comfortable relaxing. I'm happy to say that they were wrong. Once off the early-morning schedule, I slowly began to discover that when I gave myself the chance, I *did* know how to relax. And the more I did it, the more I saw how much relaxation benefits the body and clears the mind. Being able to slow down and take the time to enjoy the journey rather than be propelled by it has been one of the greatest discoveries of my new life. These days, I take the time to look at my schedule and decide what is possible and what isn't, instead of trying to do it all.

I remember, several years back, going to watch my girls practice in a nearby ice-skating arena. The music was blasting, hundreds of kids were running up and down the bleachers yelling to their parents, and suddenly I was being shaken awake. "Mommy," one of my girls said, "will you watch me, please?" I was devastated. I felt guilty that I had been so tired,

I actually fell asleep in the middle of the afternoon with all that noise. What degree of exhaustion *is* that?

It took some time to feel normal again. People told me that for a while, I would probably keep waking up before dawn. Force of habit. But in fact, I didn't. The body doesn't naturally pop up at that time of morning (or is it night?) and I had acute sleep deprivation. I started my new life in such a state of exhaustion, I had no fear at all that I would keep waking up early. Instead, I had the fear that I would wake up so late, one day I would suddenly realize that I had gotten nothing accomplished for an entire week. I saw myself lying around in my pajamas for days, not bothering to go into the office.

Of course that never happened. For a short while, however, I did find it difficult to tear myself out from between the sheets before ten or eleven and then I *still* felt tired. I spoke to my doctor and asked if I should be concerned that after sleeping for eleven hours, I still felt like I needed more. He reminded me that I'd been sleep-deprived for twenty years and I shouldn't expect to erase that in a month or two. He suggested that it might take a minimum of six months or maybe a year to truly discover my normal sleep cycle. Could he be right?

I remembered an interview just a few weeks before I left *GMA*. Our entertainment editor, Chantal Westerman, and musician Billy Joel were discussing his move from pop music to classical.

"But what about your fans?" she asked. "Won't they be disappointed?"

"What about them?" Billy answered. "I've been doing rock and roll for them for twenty years until I'm exhausted. I'm at a point where I can do what I want to do. I paid my dues. If playing classical music makes me happy now, then that's what I'll do. And if I don't sell the amount of records I used to sell, I don't care."

"You haven't made a record in four years," she challenged him. "That's a long break."

He exhaled. "I was on tour for a year and a half," he said. "Does anyone know what it's like to be on the road for that amount of time? The sleep deprivation, going from city to city, sleeping in strange hotels? Every time you leave your hotel room, there are people wanting a little piece of you. When you come off a tour, it takes a good year to recover, maybe a year and a half."

If I'd heard him say that two years earlier, I would have thought, "What a flaky musician! A year and a half to get over being on the road? Yeah, right." But now, I was acutely aware of my own chronic sleep deprivation, and it made me wonder what my life would be like over the next year. Would I sleep the days away? How would it affect me, a type A personality, who was used to running and doing things all day long? I felt like a supertrain, careening down the tracks at 140 miles per hour, putting on the brakes. I could almost hear the metal against metal beneath me, as I slowed down to 130, 120, 110.

Bit by bit, I needed to wind down and deal with the fallout of my leaving a twenty-year public position. While working the morning wake-up shift, I found that viewers didn't like to have their morning routine disturbed, so they would actually get irritated when I was on vacation. I remember running into perfect strangers who would say: "Hey, Joan, what are you doing here and when are you going back? I don't like it when you're not on *GMA*."

I'd smile and say, "Sorry." But I would think to myself, "I love the appreciation, but if it's okay with you, I'd like to take a week off work like everybody else gets to do."

Once I left *Good Morning America* for good, many people approached me with a groan, woefully complaining that I was personally responsible for changing their morning routines. They would say, "How could you leave? How am I supposed to carry on my mornings now that you're gone?" I was grateful for the relationship I'd developed with my viewers, and I understood that they were only saying this in the nicest way. Of course, it's good to feel missed, but I wondered how many of *them* had stayed in exactly the same job for twenty years. They had most likely left one job for another or moved up the ladder and taken a new position, or even moved to a new city. I suppose people viewed my job as privileged, so leaving was something they couldn't fathom.

But people didn't see that this kind of unusual schedule also meant giving up most of my personal life. It meant forgoing some precious privileges that the average person retains without consideration—like privacy. I often wondered how most people would react if they saw the letters that I received on a daily basis, scrutinizing every detail of my existence—my hair, my makeup, my clothes, my shoes, how I pronounced words, or the fact that I had ended a sentence with a preposition? Or they had comments and opinions on how I handled my marriage, my divorce, my children, my illnesses, my weight loss, and whom I was dating.

It's not always easy to be on the receiving end of this kind of scrutiny and intrusiveness on a daily basis. When I went through my divorce, I thought I had experienced the toughest possible personal attacks from the tabloids and other media. I figured nothing could ever be as intrusive and hurtful again. But just when you think it's safe to get back in the water, there they were, ready to chronicle my every step as I reentered the dating world. Prior to that time, I'd never really considered the idea that anybody would care whom I dated. But was I wrong! Now I truly understand the phrase "living in a fishbowl." The saddest part was that such heavy surveillance played into the process of whether or not I gave someone a second glance. It nearly eliminated any chances of spontaneity because I was also afraid that people wouldn't want to go out with me because they would end up on the cover of a tabloid. It's almost ironic that everyone assumed dating would be so easy for me because I was well known. Actually, that was like having a handicap in the dating world. I found it next to impossible to meet someone naturally, and I was constantly worried about my privacy.

How about just going out with a bunch of friends and kicking up your heels? It's a natural step for anyone after a divorce. But for me, it meant being labeled a "party girl." This label, of course, greatly amused my daughters. I made my New Year's resolution that year: "I hope to have half as much fun as the tabloids say I'm having." While that might be a funny line, I was actually concerned about my image. I had spent twenty years earning the reputation of a hardworking parent and a responsible journalist. It was scary to think that tabloids could paint a picture of me that was so far from how I actually conducted my life. It left me feeling vulnerable and unprotected.

It got so ridiculous, the tabloids began canvassing department stores to find out what kinds of furniture I had purchased and how much they cost. I remember reading an article at that time in which I was being criticized for buying several television sets for my house. I wonder if any of those tabloid reporters had three kids who all wanted to watch the same show at the same time.

The sense of invasion became intolerable that Christmas when I went holiday shopping in some local stores. One shop owner after another said they had been questioned by tabloid reporters as to what items I had bought and to whom I had sent them. Life changes are hard enough without the whole world commenting and giving their opinion. But I became so accustomed to being barraged with critical and intrusive remarks, I actually began to view them as an expected and ordinary part of my life. I probably learned some valuable lessons from it all, but it still hurt at times. Getting out from under the daily inspection of my every move and every word for a while would definitely be a relief.

When I left the studio after my last show, Charlie Gibson said, "Hey, we may not see you Monday morning, but don't you worry, I'll call." The weekend passed and for the first time in two decades, I was sound asleep at six A.M. on a weekday, when my daughter Jamie tiptoed into my room. She whispered in my ear, "Mom, I told him you were still asleep, but you're wanted on the phone."

In a blur I reached over and picked up the phone. A much-too-cheery voice was on the other end. "Good morning, doll." It was Charlie, talking in an overly loud voice. "Good morning, Joan," a chorus of all the voices in the studio rang out in the background.

"Good one, Charlie," I said. "Very funny, but I've got the last laugh, because I'm going back to sleep." I smiled to myself as I stretched and turned over. I was glad he had done it. It was nice knowing that someone I'd worked with for so many years was thinking about me. I think I would have been disappointed if he hadn't called.

Oh, I've got to tell you about a great "get back." About two months after Charlie's call, I was sitting on my sofa at eleven o'clock one night, watching a baseball game with Jeff. (Is this an obvious sign we were still in the beginning of a relationship?) Now, that might sound normal to most people but I couldn't remember the last time I had been able to stay awake long enough to watch any program in its entirety, let alone a full baseball game. For me, doing things in the evenings had been practically nonexistent. If I *did* manage to stay awake for a movie, I was asleep long before the credits rolled. That night, wide awake and enjoying the game, I laughed, remembering all those mornings when Charlie came in to work bleary-eyed from watching baseball the night before. "Don't even say it," he'd tell me, his eyes bloodshot from getting only a couple of hours of sleep. "I did it again. I don't know why I do this to myself, but I just love sports and there are so many games, I can't turn off the TV. Even when it looks like my team is winning, I know the minute I stop watching, the whole game's gonna turn around, so I was up until one o'clock again."

"I just don't know how you do it," I'd say to him. And now here I was, sitting and watching a game—with no guilt. Who would've ever thunk it? Not Charlie.

"Can you believe you're actually awake, watching a game?" Jeff asked me. The Cleveland Indians were playing the Baltimore Orioles, Charlie's favorite team, when suddenly, in the bottom of the eighth inning, a Cleveland player hit a home run to put them ahead by one. "God, I wonder if Charlie's up?" I said to Jeff. "Or maybe he went to bed, thinking they were winning and now this happened."

"Why don't you call him?" Jeff said.

"Jeff, it's eleven-fifteen at night."

"He called *you* at six in the morning."

"Come to think of it," I grinned, "he did." I picked up the phone and dialed Charlie at home.

You know how a person's voice sounds when you wake them from a deep sleep and they don't know where they are? "H'lo?" he said.

"Charlie," I started right in. "Are you being a bad boy, are you up watching the game? Don't worry. There's still another inning and the Orioles can come back. Oh, were you asleep?"

"Touché, Lunden."

"Do you want to go back to sleep? Go ahead and I'll call you later and tell you who won."

"Very funny," he said, hanging up the phone.

We both loved it. It was about being friends, and I finally had some time to play. And incorporating playtime was just one of the steps I was taking to create my own future.

TAKE A LIFE INVENTORY

To know where you're headed, it's important to understand where you are. That requires assessing your life, taking stock of what's in it, and determining what you need for the next stage. It was time for me to take inventory of all aspects of my life. Since my whole life was completely time-shifting, it was as if I were a different person, living in my house. Is this house conducive to this new person? I wondered. For the first time in twenty years, I could stay up at night like a "grown-up." But where would I hang out in the evenings? My youngest daughter, Sarah, spent most of her time in the family room that was just off the kitchen, while my older girls liked to be in the playroom downstairs.

But what about me? Where did I spend *my* time? I was almost startled when I realized the answer was: in bed. I had always gotten up before the sun, worked all day long, made dinner in the kitchen, helped the girls in their rooms with their homework, and then tried to get to bed by nine. I didn't have a hangout place in my own home because for all these years I had had no time to hang out. I had to create a place for the new "me" in my home.

So where would I like to sprawl out to watch TV if I didn't want to watch Nickelodeon with ten-year-old Sarah or MTV with teenagers Lindsay and Jamie? I stood alone in my living room, a room we rarely entered. It was the only room that wasn't "taken," but it was much too formal for a hangout place. It needed to be softened up and made comfortable.

First, I put a TV into a wall unit where it could be hidden away when guests arrived. All right, I had the beginnings of a room where I could relax. I would move my formal black sofas to my new ABC office, replacing them with overstuffed casual yet elegant beige sofas at home. To soften

Ten-year-old Sarah sprawled out at home.

Jamie and Lindsay pal around.

the sound in the room and give it a warmer feel, I found a large carpet to cover part of the hardwood floor. Now, if I wanted to watch *NYPD Blue, ER,* or *Home Improvement* like the rest of America, I had a cozy, comfortable, light-filled space that was conducive to flopping down. I had re-created my home to accommodate my new life.

Next, since I was living normal hours again, I changed the timers on my outside lights, which no longer had to come on at 3:45 A.M. And since I wasn't getting up in the dark anymore, I figured I needed curtains that would block out the sunlight from my bedroom windows. It was something my friends always used to comment on. "It's beautiful seeing the outdoors, but doesn't the sunlight bother you in the morning?"

"How would I know?" I replied. Actually, I still haven't made that change, and it's not about procrastinating. Seeing the sun streaming in through the windows is such a joy, I don't want to block it out. These days, the sunrise is a precious shining jewel. A bright stream of morning sunlight as it glows in through the windows may be annoying to some people, but not to me. When it awakens me, it reaches into my soul and puts a smile on my face. I feel like Sleeping Beauty being kissed by her prince. A lazy afternoon affects me in much the same way these days, when time doesn't have to be counted. Time that just slips away comfortably is a great luxury. And for me, the true definition of luxury is time.

Taking the opportunity to enjoy the sunshine.

As long as I was taking charge of my life and creating a positive future, there were other areas that now had to be addressed. For many years, like others in the entertainment industry, I had paid other people to run my business and my finances. I didn't totally understand that part of my life and always contended that I didn't have the time. But now, if I were to be the captain of my life, standing at the helm with both hands on the steering wheel, I needed to be aware of all the inner workings of my ship.

I began with my finances, only to find that the ship had some leaks. Okay. I knew I had to be captain, but did that mean I had to make my accountant walk the plank? Needless to say, I approached this task with a bit more diplomacy. I looked for someone who would work with me more closely and help me chart my course. Here I was, making another huge change that made me uneasy. "My accountant knows everything about my financial life for the last twenty years," I thought. "What if I need to find a certain piece of information? How will a new person know?" Once again, it was time to put the fear of change in its rightful place—the circular file.

I'm not suggesting that we should seek out confrontation or actively pursue it, but a healthy and self-confident person needs to be able to look necessary confrontation in the face and deal with it. Problems don't just go away if you decide not to face them. I took the step, changed accountants, and it turned out to be one of the smoothest, easiest, and wisest changes I ever made.

I told my new accountant, "I want to be privy to every detail of my financial life. I'm not too busy to understand. I want to be the master of my own finances." I wanted to be empowered by knowledge, rather than be overwhelmed by it. The more understanding you have about your life, the less afraid you are of it and the more control you have.

Next, I wanted to know that I was saving enough money and planning wisely for the future. For years on *GMA*, I had interviewed financial experts who encouraged people to take control of their lives and save a certain percentage of their monthly income. They also said we should get a financial adviser to guide us. Now I finally took their advice to heart—a great step toward creating a positive and safe future.

As I created the underpinnings of a brand-new life, not a stone was left unturned. This period of my life had the potential to be the most exciting so far; I needed to make sure that I created a future that would encompass all the possibilities. I wanted to surround myself with colleagues who truly would be excited and enthusiastic about helping me to stretch in new ways. I teamed up with an agency in Hollywood that could help me with the offers coming in. I wanted representation that could see me in a more expansive way than I could see myself.

For instance, when I heard I had been offered a part in a sitcom, I laughed. "Why would they ask me to do this?" I thought. "I'm not an actress." Then I thought back to several years earlier, when I'd run into TV producer Garry Marshall at a party.

He had said, "When you decide to leave *GMA* and do a sitcom, I'd like to produce it."

I chuckled. "I appreciate that," I had told him, "but I'm hardly an actress."

"Joan," he said, "I've watched *Good Morning America* for fifteen years. You deal with six different subjects in one morning, from hockey to health care to politics. You can't tell me that you're interested in all of them. But you make us believe you are. You bring the right sense of empathy, compassion, curiosity, seriousness, or playfulness to every interview. What do you think an actress does? They call upon the correct emotion for that moment."

Okay. Now this didn't mean that I'd go looking for a sitcom role, but it did show me that my task at hand was to change my view of myself. Not a small task. But I was fortunate to have people in the entertainment industry wanting to help me embrace a whole new set of possibilities. I was taking another step into my new world. By doing this kind of inventory, making adjustments and gaining control over my life, I felt more secure during this time of transition and better able to create my future.

Going through change feels like an internal, private experience. But when other people start to notice and comment that something seems different about us, that makes it feel real. As I relaxed about my future—relaxed, period—I remember getting this kind of feedback. A funny moment that comes to mind was when I finished my workout one day at the gym. As I emerged from the dressing rooms with no makeup and wet hair, I bumped into early-morning radio host Howard Stern, who also worked out there.

"Jesus, look at you," he said. "You look younger and more rested than

I've ever seen you look and you have no makeup on. You got off this friggin' early-morning schedule and you look ten years younger. What am I doing to myself?" He walked away shaking his head and I felt great.

By the time December rolled around and I had been on a more normal schedule for a couple of months, I finally was starting to feel human again. It was also the time of the year to dive into my yearly Christmas card tradition. My mom and dad had started this tradition when my brother and I were very young. Recently, I found a Christmas card from the year 1959.

Joan, Jeff, Gladyce, and Erle celebrate Christmas in '59.

In carrying on this tradition, I always look for a unique photo of my girls and me, and I write a poem or some prose that's reflective of the year. Since we had just been photographed for the upcoming January issue of *Good Housekeeping* magazine, I knew exactly which photo I wanted to use. We were all in comfy-looking pajamas, relaxing in a not-so-tidy corner of my daughter Jamie's room. Nothing like a little realism in photography!

As I sat down to compose something that reflected the past twelve months of my life, I took a deep breath. Boy, did I have my job cut out for me *this* year. I started out with a few trial ideas for 1997. One of my favorites was:

As you set your course for the year ahead,
Just remember, I'm still in bed.

The girls and I liked it, but finally, we settled on a David Letterman–style Top Ten list. Here's the final card:

Off the channels and in our flannels.

The 10 most important things I learned in '97

1. *Getting kids ready for school in the morning is highly overrated.*

2. *If you stay in the tub for more than an hour, your skin gets wrinkly.*

3. *Rush-hour traffic really is the pits.*

4. *Garbage men come at 5:00 A.M. Don't they know people are sleeping?*

5. Good Housekeeping *is not just a magazine.*

6. *You can't put coffee grinds down a garbage disposal.*

7. *Fifth-grade math is really hard.*

8. *"Early to bed, early to rise" just means you miss all the fun.*

9. *A golden parachute is better than a nylon parachute.*

10. *The grass is greener on the other side.*

Make it a great '98!

Joan, Jamie, Lindsay, and Sarah

Checking out what's on the horizon.

5

Remove Failure as an Option

If you believe it will work out,

...You'll see opportunities.

If you believe it won't,

...You'll see obstacles.

—Anonymous

My mom, Gladyce.

My mother taught me that life is what you make it, and if you have two qualities, passion and enthusiasm, there's no stopping you. She always said, "Joan, the word 'can't' is not in our dictionary. You can do anything you want to do, you can be anything you want to be." I only needed to include passion and enthusiasm to the mix. I took her teachings to heart. I have found throughout my life that being enthusiastic invites success. I have continuously called upon my passion and enthusiasm to get me through challenges, big and small.

BELIEVE IN YOURSELF

Out of my mother's teachings, my philosophy has become "Whenever you're asked if you can do something, just say yes— then figure out how to do it." Each success gives you a layer of confidence and makes you feel less fearful of the next challenge. It helps eliminate self-doubt, which is one of the biggest obstacles to success.

If you think you can, you can.

If you think you can't, you're right.

—*Mary Kay Ash*

One day, I was asked by the producers of *Good Morning America* if I would be willing to ice-skate live with Olympic champion Brian Boitano during the program from Central Park. They asked me rather sheepishly because they thought I would be concerned with looking less than perfect.

"Do you know how to skate?" they asked.

"Does it matter?" I answered.

When it came to ice-skating, I was no Tara Lipinski, that's for sure. But I did know how to stand up on a pair of skates and make it around the rink.

When I arrived at Central Park's ice-skating rink early the next morning, Brian Boitano asked me, "Do you skate?"

"I can stand up and get around," I said with a smile. "The rest is going to be up to you. I'll look as great as you make me look."

Brian met the challenge with a grin. "You're going to be amazed. All you really need to do is stay steady on your feet, because we *are* in Central Park and there are some nicks in the ice. But as long as you stay with me and you don't resist me, you'll be great."

Getting ready for the Olympics with gold medalist Brian Boitano.

When Charlie introduced us, Brian put a supporting arm around my waist and we were off! I repeated my mantra of the morning over and over: "If you think you can, you can. If you think you can, you can."

We skated in circles and figure eights, we skated backwards, and I glided wherever he led me. I marveled at how much I was able to do under the wing of this gold medalist. When we finished on that crisp, cold morning out in the middle of Central Park, I almost expected to see judges holding up our scores. With the rush of self-accomplishment and self-confidence that accompanied the risk I had just taken, I thought to myself, "How many other things did I believe I could do, before someone told me it was impossible?" I had removed failure as an option and afforded myself another incredible experience.

> *All things are possible once you make them so.*
>
> *—Goethe*

My thirst for taking on challenges was the guiding factor in developing the premise for my *Behind Closed Doors* specials. These specials are my ticket to adventure. I think my executive producers for the program, Eric Shotz and Bill Paolantonio, actually see me as having almost no limits at all. Our production meetings have become "Can you top this?!" sessions.

You know what they say: the difference between ordinary and extraordinary is that little extra. Sometimes when we're in the middle of taping these adventures, we look at each other as we're walking down some previously forbidden corridor and say, "How did they ever let us in here?" Whether it's the CIA teaching us how to decode secret spy messages, the Department of Defense showing us how to track nuclear terrorists and allowing me to hold deadly plutonium, or the Navy SEALs showing us how they secure an enemy beach with live gunfire and high explosives—we find ourselves thinking, "We actually get paid for this?"

*Bill and Eric
with me in front
of the presidential
helicopter.*

I had only been off *GMA* for about a month when I set out to tape my fifth *Behind Closed Doors* special. It was definitely another one of our intriguing adventures. We were allowed behind the closed doors of the United States Secret Service. Up until then, no reporter had ever been allowed to tape at their training facility in Arlington, Virginia. I was being allowed to take part in high-speed defensive driving exercises and being taught to shoot handguns, high-powered rifles, and shotguns.

Me with U.S. Navy SEALs.

Me holding plutonium, core of a nuclear bomb.

Hillary Clinton also came to the Secret Service headquarters to honor the young men and women who were graduating that day. In her speech to the new agents, she thanked them for always protecting her life and the lives of her family.

At the Secret Service headquarters with First Lady Hillary Rodham Clinton.

In the first attack scenario that we filmed, I was allowed to take part in a simulated assassination attempt where I played the part of the first lady while the agents had to save my life. I rode inside the presidential limo with several other agents. The motorcade wound its way through the back roads of the Virginia training facility. We approached one of the "ghost towns," city facades built on the training grounds to replicate real-life settings. This scenario was to be typical of a presidential "meet and greet" at a huge manufacturing plant. The crowd of about one hundred

A Secret Service agent steps into the line of fire as I work the rope line.

While I escape unharmed, medics tend to the fallen agent.

people were all waving, shouting, and snapping pictures. The Secret Service agents passed me down the "rope line" as I shook hands and exchanged hellos. All of a sudden, a gunman in the crowd pulled a pistol from his jacket and began shooting (blanks, of course). The Secret Service "covered" me and got me back into the limo in a matter of seconds—faster than a speeding bullet.

To "cover" means to actually place yourself between the "protectee" and the oncoming bullet, thus the phrase "in the line of fire." I can think of no other job where you're expected to take a bullet as part of your job description. In this scenario, one agent did step into the line of fire and take a bullet intended for me.

In another scenario, a suicide bomber pulled a truck loaded with explosives right in front of our limo. When the truck blew to smithereens, the flames shot sixty feet into the air. Another suicide bomber ran toward the car, where he detonated dynamite that was strapped to his chest. Again the Secret Service evaded the terrorist and we sped away. Each training scenario was more amazing than the last.

A suicide bomber runs toward our car and explodes. How he remained unharmed in this simulation baffled me—but he did.

As we turn the corner to escape, more explosions.

On the same program, we were taken behind the lights and the glitz of the showgirls of Las Vegas. When Eric and Bill first called about this story, they said, "Listen, Joan, we have a crazy idea. Would you ever be willing to be a Las Vegas showgirl?"

Without taking a breath, I answered, "Absolutely."

They were quiet on the other end of the line, and then Eric said, "Really? Do you understand we're talking about putting you into one of the Vegas spectaculars with hundreds of dancers onstage with feathers, rhinestones, big headdresses, and not much else? And you'll be up there dancing, Joan—dancing with all those showgirls."

"That's awesome," I said. "I'd love it. Who ever gets to do that?"

I thought back to when I was ten years old. Every day after school, I went to a local dance studio where I trained in ballet, tap, acrobatics, jazz, and baton. I was sure that one day, I would grow up to be a dancer. I must admit I envisioned myself on the stage of the New York City Ballet, not a Las Vegas Jubilee showgirl.

Now, the idea of dancing around a stage in a showgirl costume did trigger all sorts of immediate insecurities. I wasn't at my ideal weight at that moment. Besides going through the stress of just leaving *GMA*, I had hurt my neck (a herniated cervical disk) and hadn't been able to work out for a while. I had also spent a good part of the summer relaxing at Jeff's boys' camp, where the main food staples were kids' favorites like pizza, macaroni and cheese, lasagna, and baked ziti. Yummy and hearty for little boys playing sports all day, but hardly the diet of a Las Vegas showgirl. However, I was determined to do it anyway. I wanted to present myself to the public in a completely different light at this time, and doing something gutsy and glamorous

> *You may be disappointed if you fail, but you are doomed if you don't try.*
>
> —*Beverly Sills*

Stars in my eyes already . . .

seemed like a good way to go. Yup, dancing in Las Vegas pretty much fit this bill.

A reporter once asked me why I take on things like being a showgirl. I said, "When I take on these challenges like dancing onstage, gracing magazine covers, leading workout videos, or climbing mountains, it gives me added incentive to continue working on myself, stay in shape, and keep my life exciting."

I've often felt bad for women who feel they have no incentive to help inspire them. All too often they end up waiting for "the right time" to get started. I did that too, for years. Then I finally decided I had to stop making excuses and take control of my health and it completely changed my life. If you keep waiting for the right moment, you might as well forget about it, because you can wind up waiting forever. I believe in the motto "Just do it." It's important to have goals; they provide you with ways to motivate yourself and keep yourself inspired. We all need that extra spark to take us where we want to go. I'm grateful that these adventures give me the incentive to continue working on myself, both inside and out.

In order to dance on a Las Vegas stage, I needed to push my training envelope. My first step was to get back on a consistent workout schedule at my gym.

Fitness trainer Pat Manocchia says: "I don't necessarily take people beyond their envelope. I just let them roll around in it, explore the edges, as opposed to staying in one place. Then they decide for themselves how far they want to go. As people age, I've seen that they become less and less open-minded to possibilities of exploration. They think, 'Aw, I'm too old for that.' What I do is make them question that attitude. I get them to ask themselves, 'Why *wouldn't* I try that?'

"I think most people have an innate curiosity about their own ability, because it's rare that people achieve their full potential. But I'm a big believer in purpose. It's important to want to achieve something beyond aesthetics when you exercise, so having a purpose is what it's all about. It's a big world out there, so it's silly for someone to stop living at forty or fifty or sixty—or even seventy. Why would you stop? It's important to keep participating in life at any age."

I knew the showgirl segment would be a carrot to hold in front of myself to get back into peak shape. I worked out diligently with Pat during the next couple of months. We had shot the Secret Service piece over the summer, and other than a few bruises and a skinned knee, it went very well. Now I was excited about the showgirl segment—until they sent me a video of the Jubilee showgirls dancing at Bally's, the casino resort where we would be taping our show.

I watched and, for the first time, I panicked. Just seeing those lanky, gorgeous dancers strutting and gliding

Bally's Jubilee showgirl.

across the stage, their hipbones protruding, suddenly scared me. Where were my hipbones? Damn! Mine didn't stick out like theirs. Fortunately, about ten days before I was to leave for Las Vegas, Jill spoke with Barbara Brandt, the fitness trainer who had personally orchestrated my fifty-pound

Long before Vegas, Barbara was teaching me dance steps for my exercise video, Joan Lunden Workout America.

weight loss a number of years earlier. Jill told her what I was about to do. In addition to being a fitness expert, Barbara is a trained dancer. Having successfully transformed me into a fit, healthy person, she knew what I needed to do better than anyone.

Barbara says: "When I heard what Joan was about to do, I wasn't sure she knew what she was getting herself into. I called her and said, 'Listen, I don't know if you're aware of what you're taking on. Do you have any idea how hard this is? You may think what these girls do is easy, but believe me, it isn't. You really need to spend some time with me, not just to learn dance steps, but to strengthen the specific muscles you're going to need to pull this off. We need to work on your flexibility and balance. And do you have any idea what it's like to dance in three-inch heels?'

"I didn't hear from Joan until she got the Bally's tapes. Then she wanted to come by. In our normal fitness sessions I never saw her get soaked with perspiration so quickly. But between telling her to stand up straight, tighten her abs, keep her shoulders down, lengthen her neck, keep her chin up, bring her body weight forward, turn out in her hip socket, smile, and make it look easy, she was dripping wet from head to toe within the first five minutes."

I went over to Barbara's house and we danced together all afternoon. During the five-hour lesson, I kept looking at Barbara in the mirror. Her five-foot-one-inch-tall, petite, and finely honed body was all muscle, not an ounce of fat anywhere. No matter how she moved, she looked so cool and graceful. I felt totally uncoordinated, unhip, and way off balance. And yet, I had a ball. When the lesson was over, I felt both exhilarated and filled with terror. I loved dancing, but I also saw that I was quite far from being able to do what was needed to pull this off.

I got Eric and Bill on the phone as soon as I got home and I must have sounded like a madwoman. "You guys have no idea how hard this is," I told them, upset that they weren't acknowledging the difficulty involved here. "I suppose you think it's easy because those Jubilee girls make it look that way, strutting around onstage like that. Well, let me tell you something. That kind of strutting is hard as hell and these people have trained all their lives to be able to do it."

I have to assume they were on the other end of the line, thinking, "Uh-oh, she's having a melt-down. Is she really going to do this?"

Of course, I'd do it. But the more I trained, the more I understood that the degree of risk-taking is often deceiving. It's all in the perception. The perceived risk of flying in an FA-18 and landing on an aircraft carrier, something I did in one of my specials, was very great. But the *real* risk was actually very small, because I was with one of the best navy pilots in the world at the controls. The perceived risk of surfacing in a nuclear submarine and taking an island with live gunfire and explosives, as we had done, was also very great. But again, the *real* risk was very small because I was with the famous Navy SEALs, who handle guns and explosives regularly in order to protect our country.

The perceived risk of going onstage as a showgirl seemed very small. But the *real* risk was great, for no one could do it for me. I was on my own, and I would have to step out there and pull it off with no one else "at the controls." If I didn't pull it off, the story wouldn't work. I simply couldn't let that happen, so I removed failure.

> *Remove failure as an option*
> *and your chances for success*
> *become infinitely better.*

I remember coming home after that five-hour session with Barbara. Underneath the fear, an amazing sense of excitement surfaced, the emergence of a whole new personality. For the next six days, I would need to give myself over completely to this transformation.

Barbara Brandt adds: "As the time got closer, I think Joan realized that she had gotten herself in a little deeper than she had anticipated. There is a huge difference between being a passenger on a plane and training to be the pilot. She was starting to recognize how vulnerable she was about to become. Not only would she be wearing a skimpy outfit, but she was about to do something she didn't know how to do.

"Acknowledging vulnerability is the first step out of denial. I reminded Joan that she had risen to more occasions than anyone else I knew. She had shown up on the set each day during an uncomfortable public divorce and she had still managed to put on a happy face and a strong presence for the camera and her public.

"Presentation is ninety-nine percent of the package. There is so much about presentation that impacts your life every day. You can be the most insecure person but if you walk into a room with a certain presence and a smile on your face, nobody will know what's really going on inside. My job was to give Joan a crash course in how to present herself as a show-girl so she could make the person in the back row believe that she knew what she was doing. She would have to dig into her inner self for her source. Then she could take the security that she had in other areas of her life and give it a new application. This was not about dance technique; it was about being vulnerable and remembering the human aspect of her story while she maintained her pride and dignity. I knew she could do it and I wanted to help her in any way I could."

After the first session, I knew I needed Barbara by my side. "If you can cancel your life for the next few weeks," I told her, "it'd be really great. I need to train with you as much as possible." She scheduled two-hour sessions every morning and evening for the rest of the week. "I also want you to come to Las Vegas with me," I begged, "to help me with the rehearsals and the performance. I don't want to do this without you, Barbara. What do you say?"

"I'm yours," she said. "I wouldn't miss this one for the world."

For the time being, I stopped my strength training with Pat, at both his and Barbara's recommendations. I went into full-time dance training, working with Barbara for hours each day. Because of the elaborate head-pieces the showgirls wear, they must be able to glide up and down stairs on the stage without moving their upper bodies. So how do you learn to keep your head and upper body from moving at all when you walk? Well, I practiced going up and down the stairs at Barbara's house, over and over and over again. The secret is accentuating all the action below the waist. Using my butt muscles on the way up the stairs, my quadriceps on the way down, I ended the sessions dripping wet, my muscles so sore I could barely walk. Each day I improved. I wasn't becoming a dancer—that takes a lifetime of training—but I was shaping my body and my mind in a new way, strengthening and stretching specific muscles that were not called upon under normal circumstances. At the end of the week, we boarded a plane to the Las Vegas desert and began by taping the "open auditions" that Bally's was holding for the Jubilee.

Once a year a few coveted spots open up for Jubilee dancers. At this audition, twenty young men and women were trying out. As I watched one after another dance across the floor, each more talented than the last, I couldn't help but question my decision to go forward. I was either incredibly gutsy or one very dumb broad to be doing this. I wasn't sure which.

Later that night in Las Vegas, we sat in the audience of Bally's to watch the spectacular Jubilee performance. Beautiful, tall, leggy dancers, dripping with rhinestones and feathers, and wearing very little else, paraded before us. When the Jubilee show was originally choreographed and they were gathering materials for the costumes, they bought so many rhinestones that there was an international rhinestone shortage. That's how much the show sparkled. The women's bodies were fabulous. I was in awe, feeling more inadequate by the minute. As I watched the disco number, the first of the two dances in which I would be participating, I knew that I had taken on a great challenge. Little did I know that in the true spirit of Las Vegas, some of my production crew had the odds at ten to one that I'd never go through with this.

The hardest thing to change is your view of yourself. But that was what was required for me to pull this off. I had removed failure as an option. So now, in addition to learning the steps, changing the way I viewed myself needed to be my main focus. I started rehearsals on Saturday for the upcoming Monday night performance. I was working with a woman named Fluff LeCoque, a real Vegas showgirl legend, who now hired and fired and reigned over the dancers. A true mother figure, she was also a taskmaster. She and Diane Palm, the head choreographer, began the task of teaching me the two-and a-half-minute disco number.

Learning from legendary showgirl Fluff LeCoque.

Diane Palm teaches me the "moves"; Barbara Brandt works on finesse.

The first day onstage in my black leotard, I was paired with a singer/dancer named Stephen who was to be my stage partner. I learned the famous "showgirl stance" and the "showgirl dip." Imagine standing in three-inch high heels with your right leg crossed in front of your left. All your body weight is on your back left foot. Now, lift the heel of that front right foot, and point your toe until your calf hurts. Don't forget to tighten your stomach muscles, keep your chest up, shoulders down and back, your arms out to your sides. Head up and smile. Now dip. That means bend and straighten your standing leg. Now do it about fifty more times to the beat of the music. Ouch!

I rehearsed for hours with Fluff and Diane. Barbara followed our every move, learning the steps so she could continue working with me back at the room. With each dip, I was putting pressure on my left quadricep (that's the front part of your thigh). When I got back to my room that night, my entire left quad was in a spasm from my knee to my hip. In this glitzy Vegas suite, there were two "painful" steps up to the giant Jacuzzi bathtub. I had to pick my leg up with my hand to lift it onto each step. Jacuzzi, schmuzzi. I was in trouble!

The next day it was more rehearsals and the final costume fitting. A few weeks earlier they had sent one of the costumes to my office in New York for me to try on. Talk about traumatic! There was no way I was fitting into this itty-bitty outfit. I was ready to cancel the whole thing. We called their costume designer who said,

Success would mean 10 percent inspiration and 90 percent perspiration!

"You must be long-waisted. Have your ABC wardrobe person take a seam ripper and tear the seam out of the crotch. Then put it back on, pull it up where it should be positioned on the body, and I promise you'll be able to zip it up."

"Okay," I said hesitantly. I did what she said, and lo and behold, she was right: it fit. The other costume I was to wear couldn't be sent ahead of time because someone else wore it every night in the show. It was a long, flowing red boa trimmed delicate sheer cape that trailed several feet behind me. Quite dramatic. The Jubilee dancer wore it over her bare skin with a

Trying to look graceful.

few rhinestones strategically placed to match her rhinestone G-string. I added a nude beige leotard under the cape for a bit more discretion.

After the costume fitting and six more hours of dance rehearsals, I hobbled back to my room and collapsed on the sofa. Barbara stared at me. "Are you ready?" she said.

"For what?" I asked. I was ready all right. For a hot bath and a good night's sleep.

"To rehearse."

"I'm sorry," I said, "I thought that's what we've been doing all day."

"Yeah, but we have a lot more to do. They're teaching you the steps; I have to teach you the finesse. It isn't enough to just hold your arms out to your sides. You have to learn to engage your biceps and triceps, so your arms appear strong and your hands look soft."

I groaned.

"Joan, we both know you're not here to become a dancer in three days," she said. "You can't possibly achieve what these people have spent their lives training to do. But you can get it down to a point where the audience can have a vicarious experience through you. That's what we're trying to achieve here. I know you. You want to be perfect. But you can't do that in such a short time." Barbara continued: "Let's use some imagery. Remember, Fluff told you that your hands should move like they're under water, like in a water ballet. See?" She demonstrated the most beautiful arm movements. "Let your hands float out there at the ends of your arms. As they move back and forth, they never quite finish the motion."

I stood up and began to practice with Barbara, emulating her hands and arms as best I could. At least now my aching shoulders took my mind off my aching thigh.

The next day, I learned the second number. I had watched it performed two days earlier, and I couldn't imagine that it would be so difficult. It appeared as though it was a lot of graceful walking around the stage. How could I flunk walking, something I'd been doing all my life?

"This is actually your most difficult number," Fluff said. "In the other one, you can dazzle them with dance steps. But in this one, you must pose and present yourself. It's just you and your sensuality. You're saying, 'Hey, everyone. Look at me.' And you have to stand there in front of a thousand people who are looking at you. Then the drums sound and you ask them to look at you again."

I instantly saw what she meant. This was about deliberately attracting the kind of attention that makes you question your sexuality, your sensuality, how happy or unhappy you are with your body, whether you truly feel special about yourself. This was one of the most vulnerable things a woman could be asked to do.

When I tried it, I felt vain, like a little show-off. I thought of the essence of being a child, that "Mommy, look at me" kind of energy when you do a cartwheel or a handstand or try on a new dress. That innocence, that freedom, is something we lose when we grow up. We begin to think, "Oh, God, I hope nobody's watching, because I don't want everyone looking at me. I might not look good enough in people's eyes—or in my own." We all know that feeling, but it's completely counterproductive to being a showgirl. I would have to reprogram that childlike thinking inside myself.

Overlapping my thought, Barbara asked, "What kind of imagery do *you* want to use to create that kind of sensuous, sexual sense of yourself?"

I thought a moment. "I see it like a red lingerie dance," I told Barbara.

"Great!" she said. We worked on "my finesse" until the wee hours.

The next day, the entire cast came to watch me go through the numbers. That was torturous. I felt so inadequate dancing in front of eighty-five professional dancers on that huge stage, half a football field wide and more than ten stories high. But they were all very supportive, and with my partner's help, I got through it. As the production crew watched my second number, the odds shifted back to even money that I would be able to pull this off.

When the number was over, I took the mike and addressed the assembled dancers. "I don't know how many of you have seen any of my specials. They allow me to take the home viewer to places they would never be able to go and experience lifestyles that they would never know about. When I first got here, I was aware that you were all very good dancers. But now, I can see how demanding this lifestyle really is.

"I want you all to know that I'm not under the illusion that in seventy-two hours, Diane and Fluff can turn me into a professional dancer. You guys have spent your entire lives preparing for this. Not to mention you constantly rehearse and perform two shows a night, six nights a week. I understand that and I respect your talent. I just want to achieve a level of proficiency that will allow me to join you onstage so that the audience can vicariously live that experience through me."

The entire cast applauded. I had gone through all the appropriate steps with them, something I had learned from each of my specials:

Step 1: getting behind the closed door—selling the concept.

Step 2: staying behind the closed door—establishing trust with your subjects.

Step 3: capturing what is behind the closed door—creating a comfort level that allows them to share the essence of their world.

Step 4: becoming part of what is behind the closed door—taking on their identity long enough for the viewer to have the vicarious experience.

I had completed steps 1 through 3. Step 4, the hardest of all, was yet to come. I simply had to get out there and do it.

I fell asleep that night with such determination that the dance steps raced through my mind. I awakened Monday morning, the day of the performance,

The difference between the impossible and the possible lies in a person's determination.

—Tommy Lasorda

with my muscles aching more than ever before in my life. I sat up very carefully, and said to myself, "I go onstage tonight, and I'm in unbelievable pain." When Barbara arrived at my room, she took one look at me and she knew. "Ooh, we need to tend to those muscles." She worked with me for about an hour, slowly and methodically stretching each muscle. By the time we left the room, I felt a lot better.

During the afternoon between rehearsals, I had the added challenge of the press who had arrived in Vegas to catch my act. It seems that the tabloids had gotten wind of my harebrained showgirl idea and they wanted to get pictures. To avoid an evening audience full of press and flashbulbs, we scheduled an afternoon press conference.

I spent forty-five minutes onstage, in full costume, posing for photos for the *Globe*, the *Enquirer*, the *Star*, *ET*, *Access Hollywood*, and *People* magazine. I knew there was no way I would ever be as tall, thin, long-legged, or graceful as the professional showgirls. And I knew enough to be appropriately worried that the press might attack me simply for attempting this. I knew I was taking a risk; I could have tripped and they could have turned my best efforts into an opportunity for ridicule. They shot their photos, I answered all their questions, and whether it was my positive attitude or my enthusiasm, they were pretty nice to me. That was good for my spirits. Their headlines read LEGS LUNDEN. And BELIEVE IT OR NOT, THAT'S JOAN LUNDEN, STRUTTING HER STUFF.

When the press conference was finished, it was time for the dress rehearsal. I was overwhelmed, finally being onstage with the entire cast. It seemed as though all eighty-five dancers were moving in different directions at the same time. I did as I had been taught, stretching out my legs as far as I possibly could so that they would propel me across the stage. A normal step would have never gotten me to "my mark" in time and that was crucial; right behind me, twenty dancers were bolting forward, kicking their long legs where I had just been. If I didn't get out of the way in time, I would get knocked right off the stage. I imagined the embarrassment of landing in someone's lap in the audience, a mental image that was enough to keep me stretching and stepping out in time to the music. There was just so much to think about.

After the dress rehearsal, many of the chorus dancers came into the dressing room I was sharing with the other principals to give me little objects of good luck. They had watched me go through these three days and they knew I had put my heart and soul into this experience, as well as every ounce of physical energy I possessed. They were rooting for me, and for that I was grateful. When things had settled down and we were all putting on our makeup, I stopped and stared at my face in the mirror. It was showtime in thirty minutes. I was trying to control the loud beating of my heart when Barbara walked in and took my hand. "Joan, I need you for a few minutes," she said.

Visualize Success

Barbara knew that in order for me to be a success *on*stage, I had to visualize that success *back*stage. She took me into an adjoining empty room, closed the door, and asked me to sit in a chair. In the disco number, the dancers were loaded onto this massive hydraulic lift, three stories below the stage at the dressing-room level. Then the elevator rose until they stepped off onto the stage.

"We're going to visualize both numbers now," Barbara said. "I don't want you to move. I only want you to visualize, to see yourself in your mind going through the number. Imagine now you're on the elevator lift and it's rising. Ready? Close your eyes." She pressed the button on her cassette recorder and the familiar music started. I went through the entire dance in my mind, step by step.

"Let's do it again," Barbara said, "because this time I want you to be able to associate the steps with the musical cues. Then, if you forget some thing and you get behind, you'll be able to catch up. But no counting, Joan. I can see your lips moving." She pressed the button again and the disco music came on. We did this again and again.

"Okay, last time, Joan," Barbara said. "Now I want you to listen as the music plays, but don't move and don't dance in your head. Just listen to me and be aware of how your body feels." She pressed the button again. "You're on the elevator lift and it's rising. Three dancers are on it with you and they're trying to talk to you, but you're not going to answer them. I don't care if they think you're rude. You know why? Feel your heart. When that elevator rises, your heartbeat will also go up."

I nodded, already feeling the sensation, just thinking about it.

She continued. "The only way you can keep your heart rate down is by deep breathing. That's how you counteract the racing of your heart. You have to catch it immediately. Now remember, with every exhale, think of all the nervousness and tension in your body releasing. Now as that huge elevator lifts you and the other dancers onto the stage and into the lights, take one last deep breath. The other dancers are professionals; they can talk to each other and step right out there and start the moves. But you're not used to this. You'll be on sensory overload between the bright lights, the blaring music, and eighty-five other dancers. Not to mention a thousand faces looking at you, saying, 'Oh my God, Henry, look. That's *her,* right there. That's Joan Lunden onstage.' You are now going to inhale, breathing in calmness and relaxation. Now, exhale, releasing your anxiety, tension, and nervousness.

"When you've reached the stage level—once you're there—don't waste it. This might be your television show, but this is also 'your moment,' so enjoy it, because you can't get it back. If you go for the thrill of the experience, then you'll be sourcing it from the inside. Then you can let it shine and your smile will say, I AM A SHOWGIRL. Feel it!"

After this unique rehearsal, we returned to the dressing room where my hairstylist, Kristen Barry, swept all my hair up into a chignon (like

Barbara Eden's in *I Dream of Jeannie*) and placed my rhinestone tiara on my head. My makeup artist, Michelle Cutler, added more bright red lipstick and one more layer of false eyelashes. With so many dancers on that enormous stage, you need to accentuate all of your features so your face will come alive. With finishing touches complete, I put on my costume for the first number. Between Barbara, Jeff, Jill, my producers, my crew, and Fluff and Diane, I felt like a prizefighter going to the ring with my handlers. They were mentally preparing me and psyching me up. I tried to ignore the looks on their faces, which clearly asked, "Is she really going to pull this off?"

Hairstylist Kristen Barry and makeup artist Michelle Cutler apply finishing touches.

I call this my I Dream of Jeannie *look.*

Finally—it was showtime. I stepped onto the elevator lift in my fishnet stockings, three-inch silver heels, my very skimpy outfit, a twenty-five-pound feather backpack, fifteen pounds of arm jewelry, and a pair of huge rhinestone earrings. An inch-thick rhinestone choker encircled my neck, long black gloves covered my arms, my hair was pulled so tight that my head throbbed, a crown of jewels draped my face, and two pairs of thick false eyelashes weighed heavy on my eyelids.

I made a choice on that elevator ride up to the stage. I could either go up there as Joan Lunden and TRY to strut my stuff like a showgirl. Or I could choose to BE a showgirl that night. I had trained, I had worked hard, I was in the outfit (as little as it was), I had the opportunity, a rare one, and I decided the second choice was clearly much easier. That night, I would BE a showgirl.

I heard the last ten bars of music that preceded our cue. I had that "let me entertain you" feeling. Just before we stepped off the elevator, my partner, Stephen, said, "If you start to get nervous, look over the people's faces into the lights."

I stepped onto the stage and just as Stephen had said, I could see people's faces. But I wanted to see them. I was fascinated, watching people looking around, trying to spot me amidst the feathers and rhinestones. And did I mention the long, long legs? I broke out into a huge smile and I thought to myself, "Okay, the odds are now in my favor. For the next two and a half minutes, I am a showgirl!" I strutted down those stairs like I owned the place, and amazingly, I was remembering the steps. I was really doing it. I did my "showgirl dip" and my "showgirl walk." I was dancing so close to the audience, we could have been carrying on a conversation. I looked into the audience and made contact with individual people. I saw one woman with this big smile on her face, elbowing

TOP: *Please don't let me bump into anyone!*
BOTTOM: *My big finale.*

her husband as she watched me dance. I flashed her a "Can you believe this?" smile, but I quickly brought my attention back to the steps and the music. I didn't want to lose my place and get behind. I had embraced this as an opportunity and now I was going to enjoy it.

If we did all the things we were capable of doing, we would literally astonish ourselves.

— Thomas Edison

Today when I look back at the tape of the show, I can recognize a look of fear on my face during those opening moments. At first I didn't like seeing that fear, but later I felt like embracing it. The fear reminded me that I'm only human, and how normal it is to feel fear when we take risks, and how great it feels for our spirit to triumph over our fear. By removing failure as an option, I had conquered my fear, big time, out there on that Las Vegas stage.

Have you ever thought about what failure means to you? To me, it means not even attempting to take the risk at all. If I had considered failure as an option, not only as a showgirl but in other areas of my life, I could never have achieved my successes. I know that my performance in Las Vegas wasn't perfect, but it didn't need to be. I took the challenge. I succeeded because I got out there on that

I always had to be ready for my next challenge.

stage. I did the best I could. I danced around in that little outfit, and I had a ball. Maybe I even gave a little hope and inspiration to some of those watching. They knew that I wasn't twentysomething and that I was the mother of three. And the fact that my body wasn't perfect like the other dancers' allowed people to better relate to me. I was real, just like one of them, and I was doing this amazing thing that a few days earlier I wasn't so sure I could do.

Each time we take a risk and succeed, it makes our next dream or challenge that much easier. After the show, my producers, Eric and Bill, met me backstage with congratulatory hugs. Eric looked at me with a grin and said, "The cliff divers just called from Acapulco. Grab your bikini. The tide's in."

You gain strength, courage and confidence by every experience in which you really stop to look fear in the face. You must do the things you think you cannot do.

—Eleanor Roosevelt

6

Retreat Can Move You Forward

Tension is who you think you should be.

Relaxation is who you are.

—Ancient Chinese proverb

returned from Las Vegas exhausted and exhilarated. I was sailing on a high, having faced such a challenge and succeeded. I felt like anyone could throw anything at me and I could handle it. Nothing scared me—except my fatigue. That was the one thing that was meaner and tougher. The showgirl challenge showed me how much my mind and body could do when pushed. But it also showed me how much I needed to rest and take care of myself if I expected my body to be there when I called upon it. I had only been off *GMA* for about two months, so my sleep patterns were still confused. It was time to take a rest. A real rest. That had to be my next step, but I hardly knew where to begin.

Most of us have been taught that the way to move forward is to push harder. Sometimes, though, the best accelerator is retreat. Armies retreat, not to surrender but to regroup and reenergize for a more focused strategy. Similarly, when we take a retreat, we are regrouping our energy to stimulate a renewed vision.

I have a friend named Elise Silvestri who produces the *Sally Jessy Raphael* show, a high-stress television job. The mother of two young children, she was dealing with a painful divorce. She was overworked and on the verge of burnout. When I suggested that she go away somewhere and pamper herself, she looked at me like I was from another planet. "Right," she said, "like I really have time to pamper myself."

I understood. For years, I pushed myself so hard, if anyone had said to me, "Have you taken a walk on a sandy beach lately?" I would have looked at them like they were crazy. How could I possibly find the time? It had been incomprehensible to me as well.

A few days later, Elise was given a bonus from Sally to visit a spa. Because she was also given the time off to go there with several coworkers, she could do it without guilt. She spent a few days relaxing, letting go, caring for her mind and body, and getting back in touch with herself. When she returned, she said to me, "Joan, I can't begin to tell you how much I needed that. Before I left, I never believed I'd allow myself to take

Me with my close friend Elise Silvestri.

time off and really rest. But I did it and I can't believe how much better I feel. I guess I didn't realize how overwhelmed I was. Not that all the problems have gone away, but now I feel more equipped to handle them."

Whether it's a divorce, a death, a move, or a job change, they all disconnect us from our world as we know it. We feel like we're in a free fall. It's a vulnerable time, when our health and well-being become compromised. Suddenly, it seems difficult to focus and to do the most basic things. I certainly felt that disconnection in the first month after I left *GMA*. It wasn't only the change in my schedule, which was certainly jolting, but the loss of a second family with whom I had spent a good deal of

Dr. Ellen McGrath.

time and the loss of my identity. When we're not sure what's next, which is usually the case when we go through a major change, it's unnerving, it's intimidating, and it's uncomfortable.

Dr. Ellen McGrath, a clinical psychologist and an expert in the field of change and stress management, has been a friend for fifteen years. You may also remember her from *GMA*, where she has been a regular contributor in the field of psychology for a number of years. We have been there for each other during transitions in our lives.

Dr. McGrath says: "When change manifests itself as fear, you are going to have a lot of bodily symptoms, depending on your personal physical vulnerabilities. You might get sick with the flu, colds, or headaches. These are all stress-related symptoms. Your emotions may also be affected. You might get simple butterflies in your stomach or it can feel like *T rex* is eating you alive. Many women feel a variety of intense emotions, starting with panic or dread, and ranging to perspiring hands, heart palpitations, rapid eye blinking, tightening of the chest, and an upset stomach. You might find yourself uncharacteristically irritable, and the smallest of things can set you off.

"When these symptoms occur, there is a tendency to label yourself weak, but that couldn't be further from the truth. These are normal reactions to the fear of change, and you need to be good to yourself. Exercise and rest will enhance your mood and reduce your anxiety."

■ ■ ■

RELAX

For years, Ellen had pulled me aside whenever she came to the *GMA* studio, warning me to take time-outs. She said, "The pressure and stress that come from your schedule will catch up with you if you don't give your mind and body a chance to rest." And now, as I was rounding this bend, again she warned, "Relaxation and rejuvenation are more important than ever if you want to keep a clear head during such a monumental change."

I knew she was right. I think we all know that stress clouds our ability to think and act. And I've always found that accessing my inner calm seems to free me up to create solutions. When I was on my early-morning schedule, I considered relaxation to be a luxury I couldn't afford. I must admit I rarely stopped to rest during the day. In fact, I hardly ever sat unless I was hosting the show or working behind my desk. If I ever *did* catch myself resting, I labeled it laziness and immediately started being "productive." At that time, with the exception of sleeping, I considered rest and relaxation to be unproductive. I didn't yet understand that the time you most need to relax is when you don't have time for it.

Getting into the swing of relaxation.

On *Good Morning America*, I once interviewed an expert on sleep patterns. He said that deep sleep was not enough for complete revitalization. "In deep sleep," he informed us, "the body shuts down and takes in less oxygen, so you need 'rest' as well. During this resting state, you take in more oxygen and your cells regenerate and renew themselves."

I remember sitting on the set, listening to what he was saying, and thinking to myself, "I'm already worried about not getting enough sleep. Now, this guy is telling me I have to rest, too?" It was a scary revelation that I was missing something that an expert considered vital to human health and well-being.

Today, I have learned that relaxation is crucial, especially when you're dealing with change. Unfortunately, this is when it seems most difficult to give it to ourselves. When we're in the middle of transition or trauma, we feel so out of control and anxious, we want to get busy and do something—anything—to take up the space and keep our mind occupied. The truth is that during times of stress, relaxation and silence can be far more valuable than unfocused activity. We need to take time each day to let go and feel at peace, even if it's only for ten minutes. This needs to be time without any plan or schedule, perhaps before your children wake up or after they've left for school. I'm not talking about sitting in front of the TV with your remote control or pouring down a stiff drink. I'm talking about being with yourself, quietly allowing your mind to become calm. Perhaps you might take a stroll in a garden, in the woods, by the beach or a lake. We must each find our own retreat. And then we have to use it.

Not having had much free time, and not having given relaxation much importance, I struggled a bit to find my own retreat. Why did this new "free time" seem so strange and uncomfortable? Most of us are so unaccustomed to the sound of silence, it actually makes us feel anxious. We are so wrapped up in our transient, noisy lives, we give rest and silence very

RIGHT: *Keeping up with the news.*

136

little importance. We tend to just keep moving, expecting all of our answers to come from something external. But it is only in nonactive, quiet states of mind that we can find answers to the really important questions.

A few days ago, as I was driving in my car, I was listening to a song by Mariah Carey called "Hero." I was struck when I stopped to really listen to the words:

> *And then a hero comes along*
> *   with the strength to carry on*
> *And you cast your fears aside*
> *And you know you can survive*
> *So when you feel like hope is gone,*
> *Look inside you and be strong.*
> *And you'll finally see the truth,*
> *That a hero lies in you.*

It occurred to me that we are a society that constantly says, "I know I'm supposed to listen to myself to find the answers, but I don't know how to do that." All the while, we are singing along to lyrics on a daily basis that are all about doing exactly that: listening to ourselves.

I thought back to a commercial we shot for *Good Morning America* several years ago. There were scenes of Charlie Gibson and me, interviewing the morning newsmakers, intercut with Americans starting their day—in their homes, in their cars, and on their tractors. It opened with the early-morning sun rising over a midwestern cornfield. It was set to "Gotta Be," a popular song by Des'ree:

> *Listen as your day unfolds,*
> *Challenge what the future holds.*
> *Try to keep your head up to the sky . . .*

■ ■ ■

That song was part of the identity of our show, I had heard it a million times, but I'd never taken it to heart. Today, I do. In fact, I'm fascinated watching each day unfold, and I'm most definitely challenging what my future holds. Whether it's Sheryl Crow singing "Every day is a winding road," or Diana Ross singing "Why does the road turn?" or M People singing, "Search for the hero inside yourself, search for the secrets you hide," they all have the same message: We must stop and look inside ourselves for the answers we seek. But somehow we still hesitate to follow the message. What if we don't like what we hear? Many of us would prefer to keep rushing around in circles, so we can avoid relaxing enough to hear the inner messages that might call out for change.

You may be saying to yourself right now, "Who, me? I need a break? Of course I know how to relax." Well, you may be surprised. Take a moment to take this quiz that I was once given by a sleep expert whom I interviewed on *Good Morning America*.

Do I Need a Time-out?

- When I wake up in the morning, am I still tired?
- Does my energy disappear at some time during the day?
- Do I find it difficult to keep my focus (or stay awake)?
- Am I irritable? Do I snap at my partner or my children?
- Have I worried about my health lately?
- Have I avoided going for a checkup because I'm afraid of what I'll hear?
- When was the last time I did something special for myself?
- When was the last time that I had an unscheduled day when I didn't look at my watch?
- Think of five things you'd love to do but think you don't have the time for.
- Imagine how you would rearrange your schedule to include even one of these things.

I remember the sleep doctor asking me, "If you managed an office, Joan, would you expect your employees to work without any breaks, any lunch hours, or any vacations? Well, then," he said, "why should you?"

He made all the sense in the world. Why did I think I could survive with no breaks? I now look back and realize that for years at a time, I had worked the grueling early-morning shift, raised three children, and never took a real vacation. Whenever I had time off from *GMA*, I would work on another project. I never realized that it was counterproductive—in fact, destructive. It left me tired and unhappy.

I think back to an interview I once did with a local newspaper reporter, while *GMA* was on one of its road trips. After asking for my impression of her city, she figured she'd get the personal side of Joan Lunden for her paper. "So what do you do when you're not working, Miss Lunden?" I gave her a blank stare. "You know," she said, "hobbies? Sports?"

I must have an answer, I thought. Everyone has a hobby. I could hear my silence. I could have answered any one of a hundred questions about her city, her state, the current economy, the mayor, their baseball or basketball team. Why did she have to ask about my hobbies? "Jogging," I blurted out. "It's a great cardiovascular activity, you know."

"Oh, have you gotten a chance to jog since you arrived here?"

"No," I said. "We're quite busy. In fact, I've gotta go."

Of course, what I really had to do was rethink my life so that I could balance it out with some of those "hobbies" and "sports." It was a shock to acknowledge that I wasn't taking any time to relax and have fun.

Finding the time to relax and finding what I would most enjoy doing was only part of the equation. I also had to give myself permission to feel okay about it. This is one of the most important survival skills, and yet it was probably the most difficult to embrace and incorporate into my life.

For those of you who find relaxation a foreign concept as I used to, here are some suggestions:

The Arts

We can either create art or enjoy it. We can attend a concert, go to the theater, see a movie, walk through an art gallery, or visit a museum. Or we can stay at home and read some poetry or play a musical instrument. Did you play an instrument as a child? Perhaps you should consider taking a few lessons again. I sit down at the piano sometimes, and although I really don't remember how to play that well, I have a lot of fun pretending.

I've also found writing to be an incredible form of relaxation and release of emotions. For some reason, as I was growing up, I had the idea that I *couldn't* write. Clearly that was a self-imposed limitation. Today, writing provides me with not only relaxation but enjoyment and self-fulfillment.

Hobbies

How would you have answered that newspaper reporter's question? We need to make sure that we have some enjoyable things to do in our spare time, so that we're occupied with fun, stress-relieving activities. It's just plain good sense to stop and recharge our batteries. We can't do our best at home or at work when we're running on empty. George Bernard Shaw once said, "Youth is wasted on the young." Well, how about reclaiming some of the hobbies of your youth? It should be something you love: paint, write, sing, garden, sew, cook, or take a hike.

After watching my daughter Jamie learn to ride a horse, I remembered how much I had enjoyed riding as a child. So what was I waiting for? Taking up riding again has been one of the most valuable tools I've found to relax, release everyday worries, and gain new self-confidence. I've decided the world always looks better from the back of a horse! A fellow rider used to say, "Whenever Joan shows up to ride, I see one person arriving at the barn, and another person leaving." Just the smell of

the hay and the horses is a balm to my soul. And it has provided me with a wonderful togetherness with Jamie, who has turned out to be a very talented national champion jumper, sometimes competing internationally for the United States. I've also rediscovered the joys of skiing and tennis. And I'm planning on learning to play golf. It's one of Jeff's passions that I want to be able to share with him. So let's make time for our passions and pursue them.

Pampering

One of the things I fantasized about life after *GMA* was the luxury of time to pamper myself. I pondered the things I had a hard time fitting into my busy schedule, like a facial and a pedicure. I think good old-fashioned pampering is another great form of relaxation. When life gets us down, our body deserves a little extra attention. One of my favorite soothers is a long, warm bath by candlelight. You might try a facial, or a manicure and pedicure. Or how about a massage? There was a day when I considered massage either a luxury or something therapeutic only for professional athletes. Having become more active in my own life, I have come to understand the need to care for the muscles I'm using, as well as the soothing benefits of massage.

When I feel down, I think it's also helpful to wear clothes that I really like. I choose things in which I feel that I look my best, like a bright-colored jacket or a "skinny" pair of pants. And all my girlfriends agree that choosing your best underwear and your prettiest jewelry will help you feel better when you need a lift.

TOP LEFT: *Jamie and Lindsay support younger sister, Sarah—the ribbon winner.*

TOP RIGHT: *Recapturing the spirit of my youth.*

BOTTOM LEFT: *Jamie jumping for the United States in São Paulo, Brazil.*

BOTTOM RIGHT: *Don't bite the hand that feeds you.*

Snowmobiling with Jeff in Maine.

Vacation

As I was winding down my final week at *GMA*, Jeff said, "You know, you can fill up a calendar faster than anyone I know. So before it happens, you really should take a vacation." I admitted that I had never, in my entire working career, taken a two-week vacation.

We all need a vacation, even if it's a day trip to the beach or a park, as long as it's a break from the daily routine. It's not a luxury; this is vital to our well-being. It doesn't have to be expensive or far away, or for a long time—as long as we get away from time to time.

I went away over the holidays for a week with

Skiing with Jeff in Aspen.

my daughters. We were to take a short boat ride to an isolated beach for a picnic and a day of sunning and swimming. The girls appeared with huge backpacks. When I asked them why, they said, "It's stuff to do, we don't want to get bored." I hesitated to tell them that getting bored was the point. But I did gently remind them that enjoying the sounds of the waves and the beauty of the setting, not to mention one another, was what this little trek was about. Okay, so they took the backpacks anyway—but they were never opened.

Exercise

You may not want to hear it—I know I didn't at first—but exercise is a great coping tool. Aerobic exercise releases endorphins, natural painkillers created within the body, and raises brain serotonin for hours, which lifts the spirits and increases feelings of well-being. Stretching also can help dissolve tension and stress. I know that my workout that first morning after the ABC call when I was facing this change made me feel like I was strong enough and calm enough to cope.

It doesn't have to be a treadmill or a stationary bike. The best exercise for you is the exercise you'll do. If the thought of weight machines makes you glaze over, think about dancing or aerobic spinning classes. I never dreamed, during my

Hiking in Virgin Gorda.

Biking on vacation.

training for my showgirl special, that I would end up choosing dance classes as an exercise of choice. It almost doesn't seem right that something that much fun can be good for you, too.

Sleep

And then there's sleeping. This may seem like something that's second nature; in fact you may not even give it much thought. But for me, it was my number one enemy when I was working the early-morning shift. It beckoned me, it taunted me, but then it eluded me. I used to think about it all day long. What did I have to do that evening, when could I get to bed, and how many hours would that give me? Four? Five? Five and a half? Maybe six? When evening came, I constantly looked at my watch. Before dinner, during dinner. Usually it was during dinner, when I should have been going to sleep if I wanted six or seven hours. But of course, that was unrealistic. Then it was homework time. Mine and the girls'. As for the girls' homework, fourth-grade math might as well be advanced calculus when your brain is fried. I was so exhausted at that point that I'd sometimes have to read a page of my research four or five times to really absorb what it had to say.

Then came the paranoia that I wouldn't be able to turn it all off and go to sleep. And the guilt, when I was grouchy or grumpy or snapped at someone because I was so overtired. At the beginning of each week, I would plan out which nights I thought I'd be able to bank an extra hour, maybe go to bed early and actually rack up six whole hours? But as the week would pass, I'd keep track of how far I was slipping behind.

So I, for one, will never take sleep for granted. We all know that you don't make friends overnight with your enemy. Since I considered sleep my number one enemy, developing that friendship has been a slow process. It had almost become a habit to feel anxious while I was trying to drop off to sleep, so I had to get comfortable with the idea that I didn't have to be anxious anymore. My body also had to get used to the idea that it could stay asleep longer. It'll probably be quite some time before I stop waking up in the middle of the night, wondering if I'm late to work.

Sleep always makes us feel better. Without it, we become irritable and our thinking becomes confused. Experts tell us that regular sleep protects our body's natural circadian rhythms and stabilizes our endocrine and immune systems. Sleep also provides the opportunity to dream so we can process the emotional residue of our day.

Sleep is vital to healing. Our brain needs time to recuperate. It helps us feel normal again and best prepares us to meet the needs of the day. As to how much sleep we need, I was told by a sleep expert that everyone is different. A good rule of thumb is: However long you sleep naturally, without being awakened by an alarm, is exactly how much sleep you need. If you find that when your alarm goes off every morning you're feeling draggy, you probably need to go to bed earlier.

Sharing with Friends and Loved Ones

I used to have a tough time sharing when times got tough. I had a tendency to say to myself, "I've always had to make it on my own, so why should it be any different now?" Then I would get busy building up the walls around me so I wouldn't get hurt or disappointed that I was doing it all myself. I'm actually very lucky to have quite a number of great friends with whom I share my successes and my sorrows. They've been very supportive in helping me take those walls down.

> *Trouble is a part of your life and if you don't share it, you don't give the person who loves you enough chance to love you.*
>
> *—Dinah Shore*

Sharing allows us to bring our emotions from the inside to the outside. That, alone, is an important pressure release. We should all have a friend or loved one with whom we can talk and to whom we feel comfortable pouring our hearts out. This person should be a good listener, not quick to judge, someone who understands us, has our best interests at heart, and will celebrate our successes. They can also be a shoulder to cry on, a hand to hold, a confidence booster, and our cheerleader.

They should also be enough of a friend to tell us what we *need* to hear, not just what we *want* to hear. When you're going ballistic, once you've let off steam, they need to bring you back to earth. Making time for friends and loved ones is certainly as important as any business appointment or errand to run.

Laughter

I remember interviewing Norman Cousins on *GMA* years ago. He had written a bestselling book, *Anatomy of an Illness*, where he detailed his remarkable recovery from a potentially fatal and painful illness using "humor therapy." He actually rented old-time comedies including Marx

Laughing is a great way to start your day.

Brothers movies, and says he laughed himself well. I had never really given laughter a thought. Of course, I probably didn't give laughter enough time, period. I was truly astonished when I heard the benefits that laughter could bring, that it would reduce muscle tension and stimulate the heart and lungs. Deep respiration that accompanies hearty laughter increases the oxygen levels in the blood. It also increases the production of endorphins and disease-fighting antibodies.

In simple language, laughter stimulates our immune system. During the basic act of laughing, our muscle tension will melt, our stress will surrender, and our spirits will be renewed. Scientific studies have since confirmed Cousins's observations. As we can see, there is a lot of truth in the old adage: The person who laughs, lasts.

Breathing

I've found that one of the most effective ways to calm myself down when I'm stressed out is through focused breathing. I remember the first time I read about "breathing techniques." I was trying to learn how to meditate by reading a book on the subject. It said I had to start with breathing. "I am breathing!" I thought. I finally went and took a class on meditation, and of course, the teacher started with—yup, you guessed it—breathing. I actually got anxious. I better not fail at this, I thought. I listened to the instructor, and finally, I listened to my breath. As my body relaxed from head to toe, I marveled at the peaceful, calm state that came over me.

I have since found that breathing can almost always relax me and bring life and energy back into my body. When I talk to people about the importance of breathing, they sometimes look at me like I'm a little bit crazy. I know what they're thinking: it seems like breathing ought to be the most natural thing in the world. After all, don't we all do it automatically to stay alive? But "conscious breathing" is something a little bit different. Focusing on your breath as you inhale and then exhale is a great way to center yourself, to increase your state of well-being, and to release stress.

You know how it feels when you have a million things on your mind? Your breath becomes shallow and you ask yourself, How am I ever going to get through this? How will I cope with my children or the new job or whatever else may be occurring? The more shallow our breath becomes, the more panicked *we* become, until our minds are spinning out of control.

Conscious breathing is a great antidote: the mind simply cannot hold two thoughts at once. When we place our total attention on our breath, the mind automatically begins to quiet down. I do this by focusing on how the flow of air feels as it moves through my nostrils.

Each time I inhale, I think to myself: Breathe in relaxation, serenity, acceptance, and happiness. I invite healing and health into my body.

Each time I exhale, I think: Breathe out tension, toxins, and negative thoughts. I actually visualize my muscles as ropes, unwinding, loosening, and lengthening. When you find a visual image that works for you, it will help you let go of stress. We can wash out tensions and fear and even potential sickness, if we learn to use breathing as a tool.

Meditation

Years ago, when I first heard about meditation, I thought it was about shutting off the outside world. Then I read a description of meditation in a book by Buddhist monk Thich Nhat Hanh. He said, "Meditation is not an evasion, it is a serene encounter with reality." In everyday terms, meditation is about creating downtime during which we can quiet our mind's thoughts. Buddhism tells us that meditation is listening with a receptive heart. To me, this means having a clear, nonjudgmental, non-emotional view of my thoughts as they pass through my mind. It means not reacting or going to battle with them, but rather, acknowledging them and letting them go.

Here's how I was taught to meditate:

- Select a quiet place where you can sit upright but comfortably and undisturbed for fifteen to twenty minutes.
- Pick a mantra—this is just a word or a phrase. The famous mantras from Hindu meditative practices that I've learned are *Om* and *Om Namah Shivaya*. It means "I honor that which resides within me." Whatever you choose, remember that its purpose is to focus and clear your mind.
- Close your eyes.
- Breathe evenly and deeply, releasing tension on every exhale.
- Repeat your mantra silently to yourself over and over and over.

This kind of repetition blocks the brain from thinking and promotes relaxation.

■ While your eyes are closed, look for a spot beneath your eyelids. It's like a light that appears out of the darkness. I was taught to think about floating through that spot. Not literally, of course, but to completely focus on that suspended or floating sensation.

> *True silence is the rest of the mind, it is to the spirit what sleep is to the body, nourishment and refreshment.*
>
> — *William Penn*

Accepting the concept that relaxation is vital to my well-being and making it a part of my daily routine have increased the quality of my life. Invest in yourself. Don't feel guilty for taking time for yourself. You will be a better friend, a better mate, and a better parent. When we clear time to do nothing, we're taking a valuable and necessary break from work and the complexities of life. When we come back to it all, our judgment is clearer and our mind is calmer and more open. Maybe even open to new possibilities. I got a fortune cookie once that said: "The mind is like a parachute. It works best when it's open."

REFLECT

It's funny how change makes us stop and reflect. And it doesn't even have to be monumental. It can simply be changing from one decade to another. You know, the big three-oh, the big four-oh, the big five-oh. C'mon, we all stop and grade ourselves on how far we've gotten, whether we've

RIGHT: *When you think of time, watching a clock is not the same as watching a sunset.*

lived up to our expectations, and whether we look as good as our buddies who are rounding the same bend.

There I was, dealing with an ending that anyone would call monumental, leaving all those years on *GMA*, and the new year was approaching as well. How reflective can we get!

Reflection is about taking stock. It is examining our thoughts and feelings and how we're dealing with them. It is honestly evaluating our interactions with others. Only then can we see clearly what needs to change and how to take action.

Reflecting includes assessing our assets so that we can best utilize them and assessing our liabilities so we can work on them. It's an internal accounting of the external behaviors that we are exhibiting. It's getting distance and gaining perspective when we're in the midst of change. Understanding what we need and what we want allows us to look around the bend, to explore the other side of change. Knowing our needs, desires, and hopes will help guide us on our path.

A close friend of mine, Scot Evans, who, I must admit, lives in a much more spiritual world than I, has given me a lot of good pointers to help guide me along my path. Our conversations are always like healing sessions. He lets me ask the normal questions like: How could they do that? Who do they think they are? Then after some Buddha-like silence, he asks questions like: So what did you learn about yourself from that experience? Do you feel good about the way you handled it? What do you really want to do now, as opposed to what you think you should do, or what you feel others expect you to do? You know you always do best when you take the higher road. Are you on it?

Damn him! He always asks those piercing, deep, reflective questions that really make me think. What's more, he told me I needed to take the time to ask questions of myself. And to wait for the answers to come. Answers, he said, sometimes grow slowly.

Okay, so now you try it. Think about the questions you ask yourself.

Maybe you should try some of Scot's:

Are you happy with your life? Are there things you want that you're not facing? Why? How do you relate with friends, family, and business associates? Could you serve yourself better if you acted in a different way? If someone seems to be making your life difficult, could you be part of the problem? Could there be something in someone's criticism from which you could learn?

Remember what our grammar-school teachers always said: half the work of solving a problem is figuring out what it is. Most people know they're supposed to change something, but they just can't figure out what needs changing. Identifying the issues is the first step toward positive change.

Me with dear friend Scot Evans.

I've found several methods that can help us do this. Here's one that I think is intriguing as well as helpful. To get a more truthful perspective about your emotions and disappointments as you go through transition, imagine yourself twenty years from now, looking back on this moment. Then ask yourself the following questions about your present dilemma:

- Why do you think this transition was so difficult for you?
- How much do you think you blew it out of proportion?
- Did you need the applause of others to prove your worth?
- Did you need the power to make you feel strong?

- Who or what were you trying to control?
- On whom or what were you dependent? Why?
- What did you really want?
- How did you survive the transition?

When we practice personal detachment, we start to think thoughts we may not have had the courage to address before.

The truth you resist is the battle you fight.

—*David Viscott, M.D.*

Another tool I've found helpful in reflecting is keeping a journal. Journaling allows us to not only record our daily experiences but also our inner responses to the world. It allows us to review our emotions and our actions. It lets us converse with our inner self. Reviewing your journal entries will help you to develop "self-inventories" and "take action" lists.

With self-inventories, you identify in black and white what makes you happy, what makes you sad, what makes you angry, what brings you joy, what you'd like to add to your life, and what you'd like to eliminate. With these kinds of tangible inventories, it all becomes much more attainable. Here's an example of my self-inventory as I was leaving *GMA* and beginning to create my new life.

Happy:
- Sitting at the breakfast table, sipping a cup of coffee, watching the morning sunlight
- Being at home with my girls in the evening, when I don't have to look at my watch, or going to a movie at night with no curfew
- Creating entertaining television that informs and inspires people

Sad:
- Unappreciative bosses

- People who think if you're not doing what you've always done, then you must be retired or no longer productive and creative
- Lack of privacy

Add to My Life:
- Casual family life
- Active sports time—tennis, golf, horseback riding
- Professional projects where I can make a difference

Delete from My Life:
- Life-controlling job
- Enough stress to get rid of the pain from my herniated disk
- All "shoulds"

Now you can begin to look for ways to take action. For each change you'd like to initiate, begin to think of all the ways to accomplish that. Just as important as adding things to your life is discovering what makes you unhappy, so you can try to eliminate them. Maybe you need to delegate some responsibility or reach out for help.

Okay, I'm going to go out on a limb, so to speak, with this next method. I find it helpful to observe my life almost as if I were another person. Like you're watching a movie, except it's your life flashing before you. I've tried this one, and in this way I could see my life without reacting emotionally. I would imagine that I was sitting up on the top shelf of a bookcase, looking down at myself, completely detached. From this unbiased point of view, I could more easily see what I was doing, thinking, and feeling. It was helpful in seeing where I was, what needed to be changed, and where I was headed. I could more honestly pinpoint the things that were scaring me and what I was doing to make the situation more difficult than it really was.

When we look at the events of our lives with clarity, we can make

> *It is difficult to see things clearly if the shadow of doubt diminishes the light entering your eyes.*
>
> —*Sophia Bedford-Pierce*

choices more effectively. Then, in the end, we'll come out, as my mother used to say, smelling like a rose.

As difficult as it is to deal with change, it can clear the ground for new growth. Think about it: Sometimes a change is imposed on us, such as a child leaving home, the onset of menopause, or getting fired from a job. Other times, we've invited the change, maybe by ending a relationship or moving to a new city. Whether they've happened to us or we've chosen them, what if we could view the changes in our lives as scene changes? Yes, the curtain drops between scenes, but what's waiting in the wings for an entrance cue?

A boss can take your job away, but no one can take away your talent. When the curtain rises, what new role might you be playing on your new stage? I knew that although I was leaving my job, my abilities were my own, and that allowed me an immense amount of freedom, a multitude of possibilities. All the talent I had developed, all the contacts I had made throughout my career, could now be utilized in creating a show of my own. I just had to write a new script.

It also helped me to remember that everything in life has a beginning and an ending, and every ending is a new beginning. Rather than focusing on the ending, I placed my attention on the new beginning that was around the bend. Think of it as going through life looking through the windshield rather than the rearview mirror. If we do this, we won't feel so sideswiped by the random events that occur in our lives.

■ ■ ■

REORGANIZE

Okay, enough with the relaxing and reflecting. It's time to get on the stick and reorganize. It's now time to reinvent ourselves.

When the owners of a business want to grow or change it, they don't implement expensive plans without first thinking through their objectives. Reorganization means evaluating how they're currently running the business, what they want to become, and what it will take to accomplish their goal.

So I figure for us it means the same thing: evaluating where we are now, what we want to become, and what it will take to accomplish that. Surviving change is about developing strategies and reinventing ourselves. I find it's important to address even our most basic needs, so we won't put our foot in our mouth or have a meltdown. We must choose what we want to say and whom to call upon for advice. We have to pay attention; when do we need to retreat and rest, and when do we need to come forward and get going? We must address what needs to be changed immediately and, just as important, what needs to be put off. And yes, we even need to give thought to when to cry, and when to be strong.

In these first few months of my new life, I was careful about whom I listened to, since everyone was giving me advice. I also had to resist making decisions about my future too early in the game, even though I felt pressure to have my entire future figured out immediately. I had to address my immediate needs, to recuperate and reflect so that I could reorganize my new life. When we're ready to begin reorganizing, we need to acknowledge those areas of our lives that are impeding our growth or progress. I have found that self-acknowledgment is self-empowerment. It's about being honest with ourselves, which is often the hardest part. But if we don't acknowledge our behavioral patterns, how can we unlearn those that are not working for us and develop new ones? This takes time.

You can read inspirational books that will help you access the answers, but no one else can give them to you. You are the only one who can define who you are and what you want your future to be. Successful, exciting people do not get where they're going by accident. They start by deciding what it is they want and then taking action and making choices that keep them on their path toward their goals. Start by making a simple "want" list.

I scribbled one out on a piece of paper one day as I was thinking ahead to my new life, and kept it in the top drawer of my desk. Here it is:

- Time! With Jeff, with my girls, with myself with no clocks.
- Sleep!!!! Sleep!!!! More sleep!!!!
- Hang out, flop down, and watch TV programs from beginning to end (weeknights, especially).
- Play more tennis and ride horses more often.
- Take golf lessons.
- Write books and finally create that talk show I've always dreamed about.
- Give speeches and get over my fear of public speaking.
- Read even half of the books in my office that I've bought over the last few years.
- Clean out my closet.
- See some Broadway shows.
- Go out to the movies.

By the way, when I was on *GMA* I almost always saw movies alone, in a screening room (the seats may be cushy, but there's no popcorn or cold drinks in screening rooms).

Okay. I shared some of mine. Now it's time to make your list. You don't need to wait for some monumental change, which usually turns you upside down. Do it now, while you can think straight.

A good place to start is by listing your desires and goals. The more we expand our choices, the more power we gain over our destiny. If someone has broken up with you, try not to spend too much time obsessing about the emptiness you're feeling in your life. Instead, get busy listing all the new ways you could spend your time. If you don't actively reorganize your life, all you'll feel is the other person's absence, which can be quite depressing. The objective here is to occupy your mind with something else. Fill your Tuesday evenings with tennis or racquetball, take a cooking class on Wednesday, and volunteer to work with a charitable group on Thursday. By helping others, you help yourself. And you just might meet someone new.

> *Even loss and betrayal can bring us awakening.*
>
> *— The Buddha*

As 1998 was about to begin, not to mention my new life, I understood that my attitude could well determine the way I thought and approached the next chapter of my life. I was finally taking the time to relax—to care for my mind and body. I was also taking the time to reflect—to acknowledge the things I had for which I was grateful, and to explore what I hoped to achieve. In this way, I could wisely reorganize and start enjoying this new life of mine. I was ready to let go of the past, embrace new opportunities, and start designing my future.

7

Get Glowing, Get Going

The greater part of our happiness or misery depends on our disposition, and not on our circumstances.

—Martha Washington

Our Inner Glow

When I think back on all the people I've interviewed on *GMA* over the years, I find it interesting how clearly some stand out over others. I've given some thought as to what was the common thread among all these standouts. What makes one actress captivate an audience? What makes one athlete become the darling of the fans? And what makes one mom the favorite of the school—like a pied piper with the kids and a rallying force with the parents?

They all seem to have an inner glow, that little spark of enthusiasm that shines through. It's that twinkle in their eye and that infectious smile that always seems to bring a smile to the face of others. That is the most valuable asset a person can have. Our "inner glow" expresses our level of energy and exuberance for life. It speaks a thousand words. If you ever want to know what's going on with someone on the inside, just take a good look at the outside. You'll see it in their face, the look in their eyes, and even their posture. It all shows long before we speak. If we walk into a room with an apathetic, apologetic attitude, we won't gain anybody's attention or confidence. People don't like to align themselves with that kind of personality. They'd rather put themselves in the hands of a confident, smiling person with a positive attitude.

The Power of a Positive Attitude

I knew that my attitude was the first thing the viewers would see, even prior to the information that I had to deliver. Each morning at seven A.M., whether I had had an argument, a disappointment, or a restless night's sleep, I had to leave it in the dressing room. There were some tough mornings during all those years—three pregnancies complete with morning sickness and a very public divorce. I had to rise above it and start the day with a smile on my face. I knew how important it was to awaken the viewers with a positive attitude.

I'm a confirmed believer in the power of positive thinking. It's worked for me throughout my career. A positive attitude is a state of mind that we can attain and maintain each day through optimism, enthusiasm, and belief in ourselves. Pessimism is the tendency to always look at the negative side of life; pessimists tend to take negative comments personally, jump to conclusions, and worry constantly. But we were hardly born with these traits. Just as we have to exercise our bodies to have good muscle tone, we have to exercise our positive attitude to keep it fit. The results of this mental exercise are well worth the effort.

A smile is the shortest distance between two people.

Let me tell you a story that made an impression on my daughter Lindsay. She heard this at school from a motivational speaker, Jim Fitzgerald. It seems that scientists studying optimism decided to try an experiment to see if they could change a complete optimist into a pessimist—and a complete pessimist into an optimist.

The scientists went to a preschool classroom. After talking with the children, they chose a little girl who found the good in everything around her. When it rained, she said, "Oh, well, the rain is good for the flowers.

It will make them grow." Then they found a little boy who could not see a good aspect in anything—a bright sunny day to him just meant being hot and sweaty. They took both children back to the laboratory and put them in separate rooms. They put the little boy in a room filled with toys, video games, trucks, cars, everything a little boy would want. They left him alone for one hour and said, "Have fun." Then they put the little girl in a big room filled with nothing but horse manure. They left her alone for an hour to see what she'd do.

An hour later they checked on the little boy. He was sitting there and he hadn't touched a thing. They asked him why he didn't play with anything and he said, "This is stupid. I don't have time to play with all of it, so I won't play with any of it."

When they checked on the little girl, they found her diving and jumping and throwing the horse manure over her shoulders. "Why are you doing that?" they asked her.

She smiled a huge smile. "With all this evidence," she said, "there's got to be a pony in here somewhere!"

I never underestimate the power of positive thinking. According to a survey of executive recruiters at Harvard University, 85 percent of what Harvard graduates accomplish after graduation in the way of wealth, position, and status is the result of attitude. Only 15 percent is the result of aptitude or ability.

Lindsay with her pony at age 10.

If we want to be successful, we've got to work at it. I work at it constantly. The only place success comes before work is in the dictionary. I'll let you in on a little secret about the work I did to get going each day before *GMA*. Every morning, just before it was time to go on the air, I went through my own little ritual to make sure I'd be walking onto the set with the right attitude. I knew the importance of sitting up tall and projecting a positive, confident attitude. In my dressing room, I'd go through a series of head, neck, and shoulder stretches to relax my upper body. Then I'd do sit-ups to tighten my stomach muscles. I'd finish with a few leg and back stretches. The whole thing took all of five minutes, but what a difference it made!

Little girls with ponies do grow up.

Finally, just before I walked out of my dressing room, I'd take one last look in the mirror and smile. You know what they say: You're never fully dressed without a smile. I think one of the greatest beauty secrets happens to be joy! Joy is an emotional beauty that we can wear at all times.

That smile starts from the inside. You might call it an "inside job." My personal goal each day was to find my inner glow so that I could radiate outwardly. For those mornings when the inner glow had a hard time shining through, I will be forever grateful to my stage director, Patty Sheenan. She would take one look at me and say, "You know, you can start this day over at any time."

Okay, I told you about one of my personal goals. What are yours? Think about something you'd like to achieve today, or, dare I say, something you'd like to change today about yourself or your life. Think of it as something that will make this day a little better for you and those around you. Perhaps you want to stop some sort of negative thinking that constantly drags you down and gets you irritated. Perhaps you'd like to eliminate a negative behavior that has wormed its way into your personality. Maybe you find yourself constantly yelling at your kids or picking fights with your husband. Maybe there's someone at work with whom you're having trouble or maybe you'd like to be more patient with your elderly mother. We can break the habit of negative thinking if we set our minds to it and get going.

ACTION STRATEGIES

Dr. Ellen McGrath says: "You must make up your mind to be a positive thinker by setting up what I call 'action strategies.' These are ways to pump yourself up, reprogram your thinking, and change your behavior. Many people who think they engage in positive thinking often discover, after self-examination, that they really don't. It takes a lot more than understanding the problem and paying it lip service. You have to actively reprogram your negative thoughts, and then back that up with action strategies."

Here's a simple exercise Dr. McGrath taught me.

Jot down your thoughts for a few days and then look them over. Find your number one most common negative thought. Then, write its counterpoint. For example, "Change is scary" can become "Change is exciting." Now, blanket yourself with reminders of that positive thought. You can write it on index cards and put them up on your bathroom mirror, your refrigerator, your desk, and your appointment book. You can ask other people to remind you about it throughout the day.

Here's another action strategy that can help you in your daily life. Let's use the example of a mother who is unhappy because she always seems to be yelling at her kids.

First, she needs to figure out where her trigger points are. Maybe when she picks up her kids from soccer, they're hungry, she's hungry, and she's beat. That's when she's most likely to yell at them. One action strategy is for her to more carefully monitor her level of exhaustion. She needs to recognize when she needs help and arrange for someone else to pick them up when she's exceptionally exhausted. If she absolutely needs to do it herself, she should make sure she's eaten before she picks up the children and she can bring them some snacks for the car.

Second, she can affirm to herself that she really doesn't believe in yelling as a way to get things done. It isn't practical and nobody feels good about themselves when they yell. Yelling is a self-defeating action and it isn't good for anyone.

Third, it's important to learn more about how to set boundaries with each particular age group. When they were young, she could give them "time-outs," but as teenagers, that strategy won't work. It's helpful to get some books or tapes to learn more about teenage behaviors and how and when to set the appropriate boundaries. Maybe she has a friend who had done really well with *her* teenagers. She can talk to that friend or perhaps to a child psychologist who comes highly recommended.

When you try action strategies and gain some degree of success—when you actually stop the yelling, for example—you'll begin to feel more powerful. This is the foundation for the positive attitude you want to build. You might even find yourself saying, "I'm doing so much better with the kids. Maybe I can stop yelling at my husband." It all builds on itself, until your attitude has successfully shifted from a negative to a positive one.

GET GOING

Let's just go ahead and acknowledge the fact that the only person who likes change is a wet baby. But like it or not, we all have to go through it.

> *Be not afraid of going slowly,*
> *be afraid of standing still.*
>
> *—Chinese proverb*

Again and again and again. We can't always choose when change occurs, but we do get to choose how to deal with it. Taking action is a much better way to deal with change than sitting around and fretting. Worrying is a bad habit, and if you choose to waste your time indulging in it, I guarantee you'll lose your sense of well-being. On the other hand, joy is accompanied by physical benefits as well as mental ones, such as energy and peacefulness.

Between the shooting, publicity, and airing of my special in October, November, and December, coupled with the normal frenzied pace of the holiday season, the first few months of my new life were pretty frenetic. In January of 1998, I took a deep breath. As this new year began, I needed to adhere to the new schedule I had set up, to live in the new house I had arranged, and to move at the new pace I had created. Even though my calendar was filled with personal appearances, speeches all around the country, working on this book, and numerous strategy meetings with producers for upcoming projects, I had made time for the really important things.

Jeff and I attended basketball games at the high school where Lindsay was cheerleading, I worked with Jamie on her college applications, and we went to listen as Sarah played her saxophone in the school concert, and I still had time to pamper myself. Ah, life was grand! What I liked about my new life was that it was creative and productive but not so frantic that it left me breathless.

Doesn't it seem like a lot of people live their lives like one big emergency, panicking about one thing after another? It's as though they keep a constant watch for the next problem, the next crisis, the next worry. That's an exhausting way to live. I used to be guilty of this, too. I would over-schedule myself, hurry everywhere, and then feel frenzied. When you live like this, it's hard to notice the joy in each moment. Not to mention, this is how you cut your finger, stub your toe, or drop things and break them. There is very little joy when every responsibility in our lives becomes the emergency of the moment. Do you find yourself sitting in your car at a stop light, your shoulders up around your ears, your breathing shallow, your head aching, your stomach in a knot? Does it seem like you just can't keep up and you're fretting about everything? This way of thinking is a habit that can be broken. I looked at this kind of fretting as the worst

Sarah (on right) and her classmate Lisette at the school recital.

Lindsay inspires her team.

habit I had ever formed and the one I'm most happy to break. Even more than breaking the habit of biting my fingernails in high school. And that's sayin' something.

People tend to believe that bad habits and negative thinking are parts of their personality, that "it's just the way they are." But it isn't. Experts say it's a form of learned behavior that has become ingrained but can be unlearned. When was the last time you said, "Gee, things have been really good for a while. Something bad must be on its way." And then you find something else to worry about. There's a Chinese proverb that tells us, Don't curse the darkness, light a candle. Instead of always looking for something to worry about, look for something to laugh about.

When I was working out one day in my gym, Toni McGinley, the resident physical therapist, was laughing at about a thousand decibels, as she usually does. Her laughter is infectious, and you can't help but join her. Trainer Pat Manocchia remarked, "Toni has a low joy threshold." I loved that phrase! Isn't it the opposite of living life like an emergency? When you can embrace the idea of lowering your "joy threshold," you'll smile more easily and laugh more easily. You'll also find that when you readily exude happiness, others will want to spend more time around you. Maybe this is the kind of physical therapy you need.

So often, people have said to me, "You must be so happy because you have such a great career."

My answer to that: "I'm not happy because I have a great career, but rather my career has endured because I exude happiness."

Happiness is a feeling, not an outcome. If you think it works the other way, then sit around and wait for something great to happen to you. But just know, it could be a long wait! If we decide to create our own happiness, we'll be amazed at the results.

Try it yourself. Go to work before you go to work. Just prior to an important meeting, take a moment to psych yourself up and get glowing! Walk into the rest room or some private space that has a mirror. Now we're going to practice what some motivational experts call "mirror work."

Look in the mirror. Drop those shoulders, loosen your neck, stand up straight, and put a smile on your face. This may seem like a very small thing, but in fact, it really increases your "face value." Say to yourself, "I can do this and I'm going to be great! Today, I am exuding confidence and achieving great things!" If you take the time to reach inside for your inner glow, you'll present yourself with enthusiasm and confidence. Your bubbling effervescence will be so attractive, people will be drawn to you immediately and will listen to what you have to say. This kind of positive attitude attracts success. Now you're operating in the "glow zone."

This kind of inside work can drum up some action in the workplace, reexcite you about your job, and allow other people to see you in a whole new light. Everyone gets bored and frustrated in their lives from time to time. That's natural. But we don't have to sit around in our own negativity and wait for that one thing that really sets us off. We'll only end up leaving a bad impression at work and we'll go home and wallow in our misery. We can choose to do it differently.

I remember a story that inspirational speaker Zig Ziglar told at a success seminar at which we both spoke. A woman who had attended one of his workshops complained that there was absolutely nothing she liked about her job or her coworkers.

"Get up every morning," Zig advised her, "and look into the mirror. You must look into your own eyes and then find something that you love about your job—perhaps the things you're good at, things you're able to accomplish that day because you're on that job. Work at this. You've got to psych yourself up."

She reluctantly said she would try it. One month later she came back to him.

"How have things been going?" Zig asked.

"Great!" she said with enthusiasm. "It's been so much better at work. A lot of people have really changed. Like my boss. She assigned me an interesting project and she's really been helping me. And a lot of my coworkers have also gotten a lot nicer."

The woman didn't realize that *she* was the one who had changed. When she began to change her attitude and become enthusiastic about her work and more open to her coworkers, other people responded and they changed, too. But she couldn't see it in herself; she could only see the changes in the people around her. That's because she hadn't yet become acquainted with the new person she had become. She had continued to view herself as she used to be.

GETTING TO KNOW THE "NEW YOU"

Okay. So who was the "new me"? What would I be doing? What would my new life be like? It's strange not knowing the new you. And sometimes it's difficult to keep an open mind about who you are becoming. Seeing ourselves as we used to be is a common mistake for any of us going through change. At the most basic level, even when you physically transform yourself, it's hard to embrace the new you. I remember a few years ago, when I lost fifty pounds and went down several dress sizes. But I still saw myself at my old weight. When I went shopping one day, I found a dress I liked. The salesgirl asked me what size I wanted.

"Twelve," I told her.

First she looked beyond me, as if she were searching for someone else. When she realized that I was alone, she asked, "Is this a gift?"

"No," I said, "it's for me."

"Well, there's no way you take a twelve." She handed me a size eight. I tried it on, and lo and behold, it fit! I had been carrying around the visual of my old self. Whenever you change, you have to be able to visualize the "new you."

Barbara Brandt, who coached me through my weight loss, simplifies the process of visualization: "When some people hear the word *visualization*, they tend to consider it intimidating or far-fetched. But actually, visualization is something we do every day without thinking about it. You walk into a store and you pull two black dresses off the rack. Then you say, 'I think this one will look better on me,' because in your mind's eye, you see it as if you were wearing it. You place the other one back on the rack because in your mind, it's not the right style or size.

"Visualization is like a dress rehearsal as you go through a situation in your mind before you enter the actual situation. Imagine you have a date on Saturday night. As you visualize how you're going to react when the doorbell rings, you're already going through the motions of the date. In a sense, you're playacting, right down to your tone of voice when you greet your date, what you'll be wearing, and what you'll say. In the same way, if you can visualize the great, spontaneous, positive person you want to become, you're predetermining the new you."

In addition to having the ability to visualize and create yourself anew, sometimes change itself produces a "new you." As we work through any life transition, we are often forced to change our viewpoints and attitudes, develop new strategies, and accept fresh ideas. It's a shock when we realize we're different, just like the woman who thought that her boss was the one who had changed. Or when I thought I didn't fit into the smaller dress size. We are often the last ones to notice our own changes.

It's almost as if we need to meet this new person with new characteristics and looks. Suddenly, we hardly know what we're about anymore; there is this vast amount of unknown territory, and it can be off-putting.

Our feelings about the person we are becoming are bound to be somewhat unclear and unsettling. Let's face it: We've never been this person before. As with any new friend, there will be a "getting to know you" period. While we expect this in relation to others, we must remember that it also holds true as we grow into our changing relationship with ourselves.

In my case, when I left *GMA*, almost every aspect of my life was about to change. I left a family of friends with whom I had spent every day for twenty years. My surroundings were about to be different and what I did with myself on a daily basis was completely changing. It took me a while to "get acquainted" with my new life and the new me. My work ethic had always told me that I had to get up every morning at the crack of dawn (okay, so maybe it was before the crack of dawn), leave my home, and show up at my workplace. Suddenly, I was sleeping later, working from home some days, and only I knew how hard I was working. I was so used to millions of people witnessing me at work each day, I was afraid people would think I had become lazy. In fact, many people *do* greet me these days with "How are you enjoying retirement?"

I'm sure they mean well and are simply curious about what I'm doing with myself, since they no longer see me at work every day. Unfortunately, it reinforces my insecurities that people think I'm not doing as much as I should. I always feel compelled to tell them how hard I'm working, shooting my specials and writing my books.

Seven months after leaving *Good Morning America*, I flew to Hollywood to shoot an episode of *Home Improvement*. I was to play a talk-show host (big stretch, huh?). On the first morning, when the entire cast gathered together for the "table read" (this is where the cast gets together around a conference table and reads through the script in front of the producers and network executives), guess what happened. The star of the show, Tim Allen, greeted me with "Hey, Joan, how's retirement going?"

I was trying something new, acting in a role on a sitcom—not playing

My GMA *family*—LEFT TO RIGHT, TOP ROW: *Steve Fox, Jack Hanna, Ron Hazelton,*
Michael Guillen, Dr. Tim Johnson, Arthur Miller. LEFT TO RIGHT, BOTTOM ROW:
Chantal, Charlie, me, Spencer, and Joel Siegel.

myself—and I so wanted to be sure of myself. Yet here I was once again
feeling like I had to validate myself. I liken this to a mother who has spent
a lifetime raising her children. Not an easy task, one that requires a vast
array of talents, energy, patience, superior managerial skills, a tender lov-
ing heart, and the ability to turn a deaf ear, all at the same time. When
the last of her brood leaves the nest, she is left feeling as if she is a nonen-
tity. She may indeed have her days filled with all sorts of new, interesting,
and productive activities, but she hasn't yet come to identify with the new

person she has become. She only knows she isn't doing what she used to do. She is no longer "Mom" all day long. When others question, "What are you doing with your life these days? You must have a lot of time on your hands now that the kids are gone," it makes her question her own validity.

We have to anticipate this "lag time." That's the time between letting go of who you used to be and accepting who you have become. This takes time, patience, and compassion. We have to stretch out our arms to our new self. It's like entering into a new relationship.

Never underestimate the power to change yourself!

A WINNING ATTITUDE

If our mental energies are concentrated only on problems and fear, that's what we'll create for ourselves. On the other hand, if our mental energies are concentrated on positive outcomes, then we'll be in an open-minded, creative mode. When we search for solutions, we find them. That's what I call a winning attitude.

> *Nothing can stop the man with the right mental attitude from achieving his goal: nothing on earth can help the man with the wrong mental attitude.*
>
> *— Thomas Jefferson*

When we make the decision to remain lighthearted in the midst of turmoil, it doesn't mean we don't care about the situation or that we aren't committed to making a good decision. It means that we refuse to compound the problem by seeing things in a negative light. We continue to work through the situation as a person who is empowered, not as a victim. It means that we understand the value of keeping our perspective and our sense of humor in the face of adversity. Then we'll be amazed at how quickly situations will shift. Abraham Lincoln once said, "People are just about as happy as they make up their minds to be."

If your job seems dull or difficult, make a decision to walk into your job every single day for the next couple of weeks and get glowing. You'll suddenly think your boss is terrific and your boss will think *you're* terrific, too. You may open up new relationships in the office, and you might even make some new personal friends. All because you've changed your attitude and found your inner glow.

Relationships, too, go through lackluster phases. If your partner comes home at the end of a day and you're down in the doldrums, you'll probably meet him with a barrage of complaints. "The kids did this and my mother did that," you whine, and he'll want to get away from you as fast as he can. Then you wonder why things aren't going so well. Maybe all those difficult things *did* happen, but other things happened, too. Good things. A great phone call, or your daughter drew a beautiful picture. Why don't you focus on the positive instead of only dumping your troubles and worries on him as soon as he steps inside the door?

Focusing on negativity is not only unattractive but can elicit a negative mood in our partner as well. Then, all too often, we become more unhappy, perhaps we even overeat, and the whole thing spirals downward. But for some reason, we get attached to our negative attitudes and actually feel entitled to them. I remember speaking with a girlfriend about taking a more positive approach in her marriage. She was concerned that if she didn't report her problems to her husband the moment he walked in the door, she was discounting herself. But perhaps it was just a matter of timing.

She was focusing only on her problems, and the negative atmosphere never created the right time to address solutions. If you feel like you've lost the magic in your relationship, how do you think you can get it back? Are you just going to continue complaining and waiting for somebody else to ignite the spark? Maybe you need to relight it yourself. One of you has to take the first step. When your partner walks in the door, greet him with a smile, even if you've had a rough day. He'll be happy to see you and your smile, his mood will shift into a positive one, and then, so will yours. What a great chain reaction! And it all started with a smile. When you take the time to create a positive atmosphere, that's when you can elicit your partner's help and advice in managing the overwhelming tasks of the day. This approach, as opposed to complaining and moaning, will certainly elicit much more satisfying results.

POSITIVE AFFIRMATIONS

By definition, an affirmation is a positive declaration. Experts tell us that yesterday's thoughts, words, and actions have created the life we have today. And so it stands to reason that today's thoughts, words, and actions are creating our world tomorrow.

As my year unfolded, I walked through many new doors. There were a number of companies interested in having me represent their products as spokesperson. Having been plagued by hay fever and allergies that led to bouts of asthma, I was particularly interested in an offer from the pharmaceutical company Schering-Plough to represent the allergy medication Claritin. You might say I was already their poster child, with my itchy eyes and my runny nose.

I was scheduled to meet with the president of the company and a number of their executives, as well as their ad agency representatives. I was a bit uneasy. I was still feeling some of the "Gee, now that I'm not hosting *GMA*, who am I?" mind-set. But that was just residue left over from the disconnected feelings of change. I needed to access my inner strength.

I acknowledged to myself that I had a strong relationship with a large and loyal audience for two decades, which was very valuable to an advertiser.

I also recognized that even though I had interviewed medical experts on a regular basis for *GMA,* I had struggled for years with allergic symptoms that wreaked havoc with my daily existence. Finally, I had found relief with Claritin—which greatly increased the quality of my life. Talk about believing in your product. This was a match made in heaven. Now, having accessed my inner strengths, this had the makings of an easy meeting.

By going through this mental inventory just prior to the meeting, I was able to walk through the door with confidence. I could already picture the ad that would work for them, and I felt that they would greatly benefit from what I had to offer. So I could walk in there and wait for *them* to show *me* that this was the right relationship for me. It's amazing how you can direct the energy of a meeting when you go in with that kind of positive attitude. My thoughts and affirmations created my tomorrow, for I am now the national spokesperson for Claritin.

Consider the fact that we're affirming ideas all the time, but they may not necessarily be positive ones. If we're repeating negative phrases in our minds and visualizing the worst, we are disempowering ourselves on a daily basis.

Affirmations are like magic: they trick the unconscious mind into thinking the desired thing has already happened. Repeating these simple, positive statements affirms what we want to be true. It is a wonderful way to change negative thinking. Try writing some down and then repeating them over and over. They can be voiced silently or spoken aloud. Make sure you say them in the present tense, so you will hear that you have in fact embraced the thoughts as your own.

■　■　■

Here are some examples:

I am happy.

I have unlimited energy.

I deserve the best.

I will claim time for myself today.

I will share the best of myself with others today.

I will respond rather than react to every single thing.

My body is healthy and strong and vibrant.

I've used that last one a lot. I remember going through my weight loss and my physical transformation. My trainer, Barbara Brandt, always said to me, "You can't have something you can't visualize or believe to be possible." Positive affirmations set a positive course for my day. They can do the same for you. When you get up in the morning, try repeating to yourself:

Today I have the power to change what needs to be changed in my life.

Today I will change what I can and accept what I can't.

Today I will listen to myself as well as to others.

Today I will trust in myself.

Today, when I am overwhelmed by responsibilities, I'll think of one thing at a time and concentrate on achieving that one thing.

■ ■ ■

Today I will accept people for who they are and not for who I want them to be.

Today I will look for the joy in life.

Today I'm a problem solver, not a victim.

Today I will broaden my horizons.

When we bolster ourselves with positive affirmations, it helps to ignite our inner glow. Our glow begins with a small spark that brightens and illuminates our life. It allows us to plan and expect exciting things to happen. Start today! Make the positive declarations that will move your life in the direction you want it to go. If you can see yourself making a change, you have a good chance of actually doing it. Have a happy journey!

> *If you want a quality, act as if you already had it.*
>
> —*William James*

A FOND FAREWELL

8

Call in the Coach

Coaches can show us the way,

like a map through a minefield.

I knew that in creating my new life, I couldn't do it all alone. First of all, I had to decide what I wanted to do with my career. I sought out the advice of many peers in my business to discuss the possibilities on a variety of new fronts. Even years ago, way before any plans to leave *GMA*, when I was asked what would be next for me, I always felt it would be a daytime talk show. Of course, I never said it out loud, probably because I knew it would be such a huge risk, and yes—change! But the more I learned about my options and what it would actually take to pursue them, the better I was able to formulate my future.

You can't negotiate change in a vacuum. If you think you can do it alone, forget it. As much as we may want to run and hide when change arises, the fear involved makes it close to impossible to navigate these choppy, muddy waters by ourselves. We all need other people whom we can trust and who can guide us to get what we like.

Research studies have shown time and again that people who survive the longest are those who have established some sort of support system. One of the most useful tools during change is to seek out people who are supportive and helpful. These can be friends, mentors, or colleagues who will encourage us to live our dreams—people who can help us find the best within ourselves. When I went through my transition, I made every effort to surround myself with people who understood my real hopes and dreams. I chose people who could cheer me on in my successes, and when I faltered, they could remind me about what I had to contribute to the world. Coaches can show us the way, like a map through a minefield. They can help us recognize our potential, challenge us to take risks, and show us, by example, possible paths to follow.

While we're looking for people who can bolster and guide us, we must guard against those who will feed our anxiety and knock us off course. During my childhood, my mother often reminded me that misery loves company. She said to always be aware of the people with whom you associate and the effect they have on you and your belief in yourself.

Pay attention to what you talk about with your friends and how it makes you feel. Try to avoid weak, disempowering conversations. People who discourage your dreams usually gave up on theirs long ago and are looking for company. Find the people who can point you in the right direction, friends you can lean on for support. You'll find that someone else's personal experience and success can quite often help you negotiate your way through change and help make a positive difference in your life. In turn, becoming more powerful in your own life makes you more effective for others. Someone once likened the attitudes of our friends to the buttons on an elevator. They will either take us up or they will take us down.

One of my greatest coaches, my mom, Gladyce Blunden.

Most human beings have a strong need to feel in control of their lives and themselves. That's why we often become so angry when we find ourselves faced with change. "Why should this be happening to me?" we groan. When we were children, most of us were taught how the world should be, instead of how it is, so we started out with false expectations. We thought the world was supposed to be safe and stable, that it would always stay the same, and that everything would be fair.

The truth is that being in control is mostly an illusion. The world is not permanent; it changes when we least expect it. This is why, when a sudden change occurs, we are taken by surprise, and we feel rage and denial.

That's when our negative thinking can become overwhelming. We start convincing ourselves that the change will continue to escalate into multiple disasters until we have lost everything. "I'll be so alone," we think to ourselves, "and since no one understands me, no one can help." But this kind of thinking is a formula for unnecessary pain and suffering.

We need to think positively in the midst of change, but granted, this isn't always easy to do. It's common to snap when we're under pressure. Maybe we find ourselves expressing anger to the wrong person at the wrong time, and we could end up creating more problems than we already have.

THE STAGES OF CHANGE

The more we anticipate change and believe that we can handle it, the better we're going to do when we get hit with it. The best survival skill a person can learn is the art of going through change. There are some distinct skills that can help us accomplish this. But first, it's helpful to understand the emotional stages we go through when dealing with change. In thinking about my own experience with change, there seem to be three distinct stages through which we always pass.

Stage One: Denial

I call this the "No Way" stage. When change comes, you say things to yourself like, "This is *not* happening to me." Or, "I know I have to face it, but I simply *cannot* manage this." Underneath each of these statements are those two little words: *no way!* You just refuse to believe it's happening, and even if you do believe it, you're certain you can't deal with it. If it involves someone else, in this stage you often think to yourself: "No way *I'm* gonna change, so *you* change."

■ ■ ■

Stage Two: Uncertainty

This stage is all about ambivalence: "Yes, I can" is quickly followed up by "No, I can't." "No, I won't" is stepping on the heels of "Yes, I will." As if we were riding an emotional roller coaster, we go through extreme ups and downs, generated by a great deal of fear. Understand that fear is a normal part of the process. We need to acknowledge it and talk about it before we can move on to the final stage of accepting change.

Stage Three: Acceptance

Once we have come out of denial and uncertainty enough to evaluate what the change looks like, we can decide what we need to do about it. This is the point where we have accepted the inevitability of the change. Now we can begin to build the skills that we need to manage it. We are ready to take charge of our lives, look for resources, and set up the appropriate steps to meet our goals. This stage means taking action. It can also mean reaching out for help. It's time to call in the coach.

FINDING A COACH

Someone else's personal experience and success can help us negotiate our way through change and help make a positive difference. We all have role models, people whom we look to and admire, people who are accomplishing what we'd like to accomplish, and have already successfully reinvented themselves. Take a few minutes to make a list of people who come to mind in your life. Now it's time to pick up the phone and make the call. Why do we find it so difficult to ask for help? The truth is that most people view asking for help as a sign of weakness or an imposition on others. Before we even pick up the phone, we've usually convinced ourselves that the other person will most certainly say no and will politely find a way out. And heaven forbid they should be left thinking,

"If she was really smart and talented, she wouldn't need to be asking for help."

But what we're really exhibiting is a willingness and a desire to grow and learn. We're also showing our trust in another person to help us. When we deny someone the opportunity to help us because we don't want to "bother" them, we take away their chance to contribute to our lives. Sometimes we need help in seeking out new solutions and strategies. And let's face it—sometimes we also need some hand-holding and consoling.

There are times when life changes right underneath your nose. One day your child thinks you are a superhero. You can do no wrong, you know everything, and they'll do anything you ask. All of a sudden, they become—dare I say it—teenagers. Aaarghhhh! Now you're a moron, unhip, uninformed, and whatever you ask, they deliberately do the opposite. When this happens, why does it always seem like we're the only ones? Instead of viewing this as a natural change that we should have anticipated, we take it as a personal failure as a parent.

Did your teenage daughter dye her hair pink like mine did? Believe it or not, you're not alone. When you start talking to other parents, you'll usually discover that whatever is happening to you is quite often happening to them. It helped put things into perspective when I found out that a friend's son had his ear and his navel pierced when he was fifteen, and she had to look at orange hair for six months. It was also consoling to learn that today that same teenager has become a successful businessman with a healthy, happy family. At points of vulnerability, when life deals us a new hand, we must reach out, voice our fears, and ask for help.

A few days ago, I got a phone call from a friend who is experiencing traumatic change in several major areas of her life. While she was going through a divorce, things started to change in her office as well. At first, I hardly knew who was calling, because her voice was so breathy and panicky. When I realized who it was, I knew immediately I needed to drop my plans and meet her for lunch.

When she walked into the restaurant and first saw me, she burst into tears. This emotional release alone was therapeutic. As she poured her heart out, I listened without judging or jumping in. We sorted through the issues, and I noticed that with each crisis she laid out (and they were all crises), she was taking them personally. The departure of coworkers to her represented abandonment. She was viewing opportunities opening up as opportunities missed. With each passing minute, she was building mountains out of molehills.

I worked with her to unravel the knots. I tried to help her see that coworkers leaving for other opportunities had nothing to do with her. As far as opportunities missed, as long as she kept her eye on the ball and didn't allow herself to be distracted by her emotions, her talent was her greatest strength. If she showed up as a shining star in the midst of her chaotic office, she would be noticed. And then came my real challenge— to tell a friend what she needed to hear, not necessarily what she wanted to hear.

I pointed out to her that it was not the time to march in, give them a piece of her mind, and demand a bigger piece of the action. With her office in such a state of turmoil, timing was everything. I reminded her that at this juncture, her best insurance policy was to be part of the solution, not part of the problem. I saw her face relax, her eyes brighten, and her shoulders drop as we started brainstorming about suggestions she could take to her bosses. By the time we left the restaurant, she had a plan of action and a list of potential candidates in mind for those abandonments—oops, now they had become openings—at her office. She had brought out her fears, insecurities, and emotions and we had dealt with them together. Now, she was viewing the changes in her life as opportunities instead of problems. Incidentally, this same friend had been there for me, time and again, to provide comfort and help coach me through my divorce.

We all need caring friends who know how to listen, people who offer us the strength we need to build our confidence and the guidance to help keep us on the path when the going gets rough. This is where coaches come in. When I refer to coaches, I don't mean we necessarily have to hire a professional, an expensive therapist, or a consultant to be our coach. You can recruit a friend, neighbor, or colleague who has certain skills that you don't have. And perhaps you can even offer to help out that person in exchange. When you take turns, the two of you ultimately will help open each other's minds to new kinds of possibilities that weren't previously in your individual realms. This can be extremely empowering, because not only do you get help, you also have the opportunity to give something back. That in itself is strengthening.

The best way to find a coach is to do a relationship inventory. Look first at your inner circle for the people you know who could be potential coaches and supporters. If nobody has the particular skill base that you need, then look outside of that circle. Does anyone have what you need in the next tier of your friends and acquaintances?

Research suggests that when a major crisis occurs, it could easily take from three to four months to get past self-blame, denial, emotional vulnerability, and the impulse to sell ourselves short. As a rule of thumb, it will usually take nine months or more before we are on the other side, so choose a coach who will have the time and commitment to see you all the way through. By the way, it won't work if you sit around and wait for someone to come and rescue you. You're the one who needs help immediately, so you need to be the one to reach out. When you find the person who can help, actively reach out. "Can you coach me?" you ask. It's that simple.

Effective coaching has two parts. The first is dealing with your feelings in a safe environment where you don't have to edit yourself. The second is coming up, once again, with "action strategies." As with everything in life, it isn't enough just to talk. You have to act. In certain cases, you may find that there is no one you know who has the skill base to help you. Perhaps you're in the midst of a change that is so debilitating, you absolutely need professional help. Large changes, particularly loss, can leave you overwhelmed, with feelings of insecurity and the sense that you can't cope. You may find yourself in a funk or a crisis that could last from one to seven days. If it lasts longer than two weeks, you may have a clinical condition and need professional help. All too often, people experiencing severe blues during transition don't seek help because they view it as a weakness and they're afraid they'll be stuck in therapy for life. This isn't usually the case. In most instances, seeing a mental health professional from one to four times can be extremely helpful in reducing feelings of depression and getting you moving again. It usually won't take longer than that to regain control and happiness.

When a close friend of mine died on the TWA Flight 800 plane crash off the coast of Long Island, New York, days went by and I couldn't seem to ease the pain. I realized I needed someone with skills and knowledge that I didn't have, someone who could offer me intelligent guidance. So I sought out a psychologist who specialized in grief counseling. We only spent a few hours together, but it helped me sort out my feelings. With her keen ability to listen and a few insightful comments, I actually ended up guiding *myself* through it. While speaking to this wise woman about my feelings, I saw that this death had triggered a childhood trauma that I never had healed: the loss of my father in a plane crash.

In one session, I was able to sort through my emotions and understand that I was dealing with more than the death of my friend. I also had some unfinished business with my father's death. The first order of business was to attend the funeral of my friend, Jed Johnson. He had been a quiet and unassuming young man who had actually accomplished a great deal and left his mark on the design industry. As I listened to the eulogies, I celebrated his aliveness, and was able to bring my own closure and meaning to his life. Now, I wanted to do the same with my father. That weekend, I drove out to the beach on Long Island where the TWA plane had crashed just offshore. I took off my shoes and walked along the sandy beach, allowing the waves to splash on my legs. There, I reflected on all the lives my father had saved, the new babies he had brought into the world, and the new technologies he had helped to create in the field of cancer surgery. I also thought about all the people who would benefit from the hospitals he built, and all the joy he had brought to my mom, my brother, and me. I expressed my gratitude for his inspiration and guidance. I said my good-byes. A calmness came over me, I sighed relief, and although I would always miss my father, I felt that my burden had been lifted.

I learned from this psychologist that past losses that haven't been dealt with often get reactivated by a present event. Experts call it "the rekindling effect." When this occurs, talking to a skilled counselor is important. If you had a sprained ankle, would you go talk to your friend about it and let it heal itself? No, you'd go see a doctor who specializes in bones. But for some reason, we've been programmed to believe that emotional pain is not as valid as physical pain. This is a highly impractical attitude that we need to change. Life is far too overwhelming without help.

My first coach—my dad, just before he died.

TAKING ACTION

One of the greatest antidotes to fear and anxiety is action. During change, taking action is the quickest and most effective way to own our strength. In order to get through change effectively, we must be proactive in our intentions, rather than reactive to the intentions of others. So when we've found our coach, we devise our new strategies and goals from a sense of possibilities, not fear. It isn't enough just to talk; we need to take action.

Dr. McGrath says: "Action plus energy equals power. You must take action, even if it's the smallest of steps. If you can't figure out what you want to do, get a creative friend to coach you about taking action. When you feel alone, inadequate, weak, or afraid of change, ask yourself what's good about you. Why would you abandon what has already gotten you this far? Try to utilize your qualities in a new way, and you'll be guiding yourself toward a goal.

"As you come up with strategies for change, talk them over with your coach—not just for approval, but to see for yourself whether or not you are making sense. It will also help you break down your goal into small, doable steps. You reach out, you talk to the coach, you get encouragement, and you start exercising whatever you and your coach come up with."

I often find myself sharing information about the stages of parenting with other moms. And quite often, I've gotten valuable guidance from watching others. Just recently, Barbara Brandt told me that by seeing other mothers feel sad when their children went off to school, she learned the importance of preparing for upcoming stages. Her youngest daughter is turning five, and she'll be going to kindergarten next year. Barbara told me she's being proactive; although there are many months before her daughter will be gone from the home for several hours a day, she's already planning ways to fill that time. She's preparing now for a future change so the absence won't suddenly take her by surprise. She's already laying the groundwork, allying herself with a charitable program that helps inner-city youths build self-esteem. She's using what she's got—her dance training. These children, who would otherwise find themselves on the streets, will, with Barbara's help, be on a stage performing. Her excitement about this prospect will fill any emptiness she might have encountered.

Barbara knows what she needs to do, but more often than not, we need help in seeking out new solutions and new strategies. We need consoling and hand-holding—just like your parents gave you when you were a little child facing something scary. The idea is to talk about your worries and explore attributes, and then use those attributes as a bridge to the outside world.

Maybe you've decided to go back to school, get a part-time job, take up a sport, or involve yourself in a charity. When you're changing your identity, as in the "empty nest syndrome," when your children are all gone, it's important to get back into the real world. You don't want to wait until your children leave and you're left feeling heartbroken. You want to be able to say good-bye, then turn right around and go to your first class in gardening. You'll soon understand how the parts of you that worked so well as a mother are still there. They just need to be tested in a new environment.

While others suggested that I take a year off after *GMA*, I knew myself well enough to know that that was not the environment in which I would best thrive. Several months prior to my departure from *GMA*, I signed a deal with William Morrow to write this book. While I was finding my way in my new life, it gave me a new challenge in which I could incorporate all that was happening. I reached out for coaches to offer me advice and support that I could use on two fronts: real life and the printed page. You're hearing from some of those coaches throughout these pages, and of course, there are many other unsung heroes who have contributed on a more personal level. I found it a bit difficult to ask for help in the beginning, but it got easier as time passed. That was because when I did reach out for help, people were usually thrilled to be asked for advice and to be able to offer me help. I attribute much of my success in sailing through this transition, and creating such an exciting and satisfying new life, to calling in my coaches. I thank them all.

It's a wonderful feeling to be able to offer support and guidance to others. Just a few days before Charlie Gibson's final day on *GMA* in the spring of 1998, we got together for breakfast with some of the studio crew. When asked how he was dealing with his imminent departure, he said he was grieving over the loss of something that had meant so much to him and had been such an important part of his life. He said that he felt disconnected and a little dubious about the future, even though he was already scheduled to anchor a prime-time newsmagazine show in the fall for ABC. Oh, he was feeling that trauma called change about which we've been talking. I heard it in his words, I saw it on his face, I felt it in his demeanor. I wanted to reach out and hold his hand, but all the guys were there. I did assure him, though, that while change was disconcerting, life on the other side was fabulous! We spoke about how his body might react to a later wake-up time, and what he could anticipate. While I extolled the virtues of sleep, sleep, and more sleep, I also encouraged him to fill up some of his empty time, perhaps with sailing, which he loves, or golf, which he wants to improve, so his loss wouldn't be so palpable.

Two days later, May 1, 1998, we all gathered at Tavern on the Green in New York City's Central Park, from which his final show was broadcast. We knew it would be a three-hankie show 'cause he's such a sentimental guy. I had steeled myself for my final broadcast, determined to make it a celebration. I had felt obligated to keep it together for everyone. But at his show, forget about it! I cried more on his final show than I did on my own. We all did. But at the same time, being able to walk on that set so comfortably ensconced in my new life, feeling whole, and being able to extend a hand to Charlie completed my own circle of change. I had made it around the bend. Now I could be the coach.

RIGHT: *We all say a fond farewell to Charlie on his last day at* GMA.

9

Don't Burn Bridges

Beware of burning bridges.
You never know how many
times you'll have to cross the
same river.

Life isn't always fair. We can play by all the rules in the book, but chances are we're still going to encounter disappointment along the way. We may not have done anything wrong; we may not have invited the situation. But bad things do happen to good people. How we cope with the tough times will not only affect the outcome of that situation but will have an impact on how we are able to cope with difficult times in the future. Our measure of character lies in how we deal with that unfairness.

I learned a lot about coping and surviving while dealing with this last transition. I knew that the way in which I handled my departure would greatly impact what I could do with my future. While it was uncomfortable to feel millions of eyes upon me, it did inspire me to gently and gratefully close one door and step through another, into a new world. Handling life's changes effectively can open doors, broaden your opportunities, and give you a chance to make your dreams come true. When you burn your bridges, you close doors.

Sometimes it seems like the whole world is dumping on you. Some people assume that everything that happens is their fault. These people are called "hypervigilant," constantly surveying life in preparation for the next catastrophe. Remember, it's not always about you. If we can let go of our need to always have to explain ourselves, and always have to be understood or validated, we'll find it much easier to avoid losing our temper and resorting to attack with a thoughtless remark. Attacking in the heat of frustration can win the battle, but we'll probably lose the war in the end.

I remember being told at a very young age, "You may please some of the people some of the time, but you're never going to please all of the people all of the time." For a long time, I must admit I tried. Having to deal with the disapproval of others can be extremely uncomfortable, but at times, it's unavoidable. However, as soon as we accept the fact that we're not going to get the approval of everyone, life becomes much easier.

When we leave jobs, friendships, and relationships, there's usually someone out there who leaves us with a stomachache. We've probably had that moment when all we can think about is blowing that other person out of the water, so we'll come out looking like we're right. I'm going to share with you an image that I have often used when dealing with these types of situations. I think of these words: Don't insult the crocodile until you've crossed the river. It's such a vivid image, one that reminds me to hold my tongue when I'm about to blurt out something that will inevitably come back to bite me. Ah, yes. I find that image of the crocodile very effective in getting across the river. Then of course, when we're standing on the other side of the river, the fantasy is to blow up the bridge. We want to cut ourselves loose from any of the bad or hurt feelings associated with the situation: we don't want to see, talk to, or think about the people involved ever again.

Stop! Before you push the button, remember a nugget of wisdom that has served me well: don't burn bridges. You never know how many times you'll have to cross the same river. From the time I was a very little girl, my mother always told me not to burn my bridges behind me. She said if I did, I'd be sorry later. I was very little and what I misheard her say was, "Don't burn your britches behind you." I never questioned it; you don't question your parents when you're that young. But even though I heard it wrong, I got the point, anyway. In fact, I had a vivid image of my little Carter's ablaze behind me if I blurted out my anger without thinking. That was an image that worked better than my mother could ever have imagined. But she did think it was pretty funny a number of years later when she heard me repeat my version of her philosophy. Britches, bridges. Any way you look at it, it's a bad idea to burn anything that'll burn you back.

About six months after leaving *GMA*, I traveled back to Las Vegas to shoot another segment for *Behind Closed Doors*. We went behind the doors of Controlled Demolition, Inc., the experts in the field of imploding buildings. There is an art to strategically placing dynamite and weakening the infrastructure of a building so that it can be brought down within its own footprint. They are able to take down skyscrapers in downtown areas, miraculously not damaging surrounding buildings. We've probably all seen these implosions on the news from time to time, but how do they do it? That's what we set off to discover. In my usual participatory fashion, I got to help place the dynamite. Then the ultimate. I got to push the button and blow up the legendary Aladdin Hotel on the Vegas strip. In a matter of seconds, the twenty-story structure was reduced to a heap of rubble. I thought it was kind of ironic that I had made it through these last six months of changes without burning or blowing up any bridges, and now I was blowing up an entire hotel! The difference here was that this was not destructive. We were responsibly paving the way for positive change, creating room for new business and new jobs. Interestingly, I thought that this unique opportunity would allow me to vent some aggression. Lots of people had said to me, "What an opportunity. I hope you have someone in mind when you push that button so you can blow them to smithereens."

But you know what? I didn't. It was a free feeling to know that there was no one I wanted to annihilate. I only thought about how cool it was to be able to effect such a huge change in a matter of seconds. God, wouldn't it be great if all of life was this way?

■ ■ ■

TOP LEFT: *Me with Stacey Loiseaux before blowing up the hotel.*
TOP RIGHT: *Explosion of the Aladdin Hotel.*
BOTTOM LEFT: *The cloud of smoke after the hotel exploded.*
BOTTOM RIGHT: *Standing in the rubble after the explosion.*

TAKING RESPONSIBILITY
FOR YOUR ACTIONS

Have you ever noticed how blaming others actually requires a lot of mental energy? It stirs up stress and unhappiness. And when we blame our unhappiness on others, it renders us powerless, because in essence, we're saying that our happiness is dependent upon the actions or approval of others. That means it's not under our control. When we stop blaming others and start taking responsibility, we take back control and power over our own happiness.

When someone renders an opinion about us, it probably has some merit. Rather than criticizing it, we would be better served if we took some time to think about it. We often get so caught up in defending ourselves that we are battle-bound and blind to any truths that may reside in these criticisms of us. But what is being rendered is an opinion or observation about us, our actions or our thoughts. Reaction to criticism is usually defensive because we often feel attacked, and in fact, we probably feel the need to defend or counterattack.

Taking responsibility for our actions allows us to own our behaviors, actions, and thoughts. When we own them, we can change them. When the panic wanes, and we're able to focus on solutions, we can also take a moment to learn from the incident. We need to stop blaming others long enough to see what actions of ours might have contributed to the crisis. Maybe you lost your enthusiasm at work. Maybe you weren't performing up to your potential. Maybe you were picking fights with your partner. Maybe you were down in the dumps, acting negative and depressed and therefore inattentive.

Most of us would say that stress and anxiety are in most part due to our problems in dealing with change in our lives. Actually, it's how we relate and react to these problems. We can view them simply as crises, or we can view them as learning opportunities. Could these situations perhaps teach us to be more patient, more considerate, more conscientious and forgiving? Sometimes it can even be helpful to outwardly agree with the criticism directed toward us. When we relinquish the need to be right and stop needing to look like the winner, we can diffuse the crisis. When we give the other person the benefit of the doubt, we disown the need to win. This can be very freeing. The immediate result is that we replace that need to be right with a restored sense of calm. We may also improve our chances of coming to a peaceful resolution with the other person.

It's very helpful to keep in mind that in any crisis, other people are most likely dealing with their own problems. They're not usually out to get us and make our lives miserable (a pretty self-centered viewpoint, anyway). Perhaps they had unrealistic expectations that we never could have met anyway. So in that case, the crisis is not about us. It's about them. This is about having compassion for the other person, which allows us an opportunity to learn something about ourselves.

It may seem difficult not to react when someone tosses negativity in our direction. But remember, just because somebody throws us the ball, it doesn't mean we have to catch it. When someone throws us a comment that is negative, it's our choice whether we catch it and feel hurt or angry—or whether we drop it and go on with our day. What's more important? To react to every comment that comes our way, or not to catch the ball at all, thereby protecting our emotional well-being?

The less compelled we are to prove ourselves right, the easier it becomes to step back from the fracas and keep our focus. Others will note our confidence and inner calm, and might even follow our example.

LEAVE A GOOD IMPRESSION

When we remain calm and focused on positive solutions rather than try-ing to prove ourselves right, we're able to operate from a position of strength. When we are cool and unflappable, we cannot be prodded or goaded into a showdown. Refusing to be drawn into an emotional argument can increase our odds of staying on top of a situation.

It's also not a good idea to be tempted by coworkers and friends to divulge or dump our emotions on them when we're in crisis. If you've been reprimanded, demoted, transferred, passed over, or let go, don't bad-mouth the bosses or the company. You can almost bet it will get back to them. If you're tempted to gossip, just remember, you never know if the person to whom you're gossiping will one day be the person to whom you have to report. I always think about something a friend once told me: "The toes you step on today may be connected to the butt you have to kiss tomorrow."

Our parting words, whether in a personal relationship or a professional setting, will leave an impression that might come back to haunt us. They may indeed be the words we have to eat later. How people perceive us may have an impact on how we make it through our transition. If you leave a bad impression with your boss, how can you be sure that person will never again be in a position of authority over you? Do you want someone talking or thinking ill of you? When you go to apply for your next job, do you want to have to worry what they might find when they call your last job for references?

On a more personal level, what if you meet someone that you really like? But before it gets off the ground, it turns out they coincidentally know the person that you just broke up with, or should I say blew up with. Wouldn't it have served you better to have relinquished the need to have the last word, to look like the winner? Wouldn't it have been better to have left the bridge standing and to have left a good impression?

I remember, twenty years ago, when I was leaving KCRA-TV in Sacramento, California, where I had started in television, to come to New York City. I had been offered a job to report and anchor at WABC-TV, the ABC affiliate in the number one market in the country. It was an opportunity too good to refuse. However, my soon-to-be-ex-boss didn't exactly see it that way, since the newscast that I was on was number one in Sacramento. His initial reaction was to say in front of a lot of my associates, "You'll be back in six months on your knees, begging for your job back."

As much as that stung, somehow I resisted the urge to react to those words. I chose not to burn a bridge. After all, his station gave me my first break in TV, and he may well have thought I should have gone to him for advice before making a major move. So I thanked him for all that I had learned while working at his station. As a relative newcomer to the industry, I felt it was far more important to show my gratitude and leave a good impression as I rounded this bend. I don't know where I got the good sense, but boy, am I glad I did. It turns out that I have needed that station's cooperation from time to time in obtaining footage of my early career. And you never know, I might be doing a show in the future that I'll want to sell to them.

Also, by thanking him and acknowledging the station's contribution in my getting the job in New York, I left him with "bragging rights." This was a much wiser choice as I flew off to my new post in the Big Apple. Some years later, when I left WABC to take the job as host of *Good Morning America*, again I encountered a negative reaction.

About a month after I made the move to the network, I heard that the WABC news director was saying, "It's a good thing Joan got the gig at *GMA*, because I was going to fire her anyway."

There may have been any number of reasons why this man chose to react in this way. I've actually found it helpful to write down the possible reasons for someone's negative reactions. It can sometimes help you see more clearly what's really happening and you can learn a lot about yourself. This type of exercise can help you gain more control and, more important, it can teach you not to take every negative comment personally. Let's use the case of the news director and examine the possible reasons for his negative reaction.

1. Quite often local affiliates can feel like a network is "harvesting the fruit off the vine"—taking talent they trained and nurtured.
2. He had recently arrived at WABC-TV, and I wasn't one of "his picks." Maybe he wanted to bring in one of his own "finds" whom he could mold.
3. Maybe I just rubbed him the wrong way.
4. Maybe since I had been dividing my time between WABC and *GMA* for the past year, he may have felt that I lost my enthusiasm, and was questioning my loyalty to the station.
5. Maybe, in his opinion, I just wasn't the right reporter for that station at that time.

Whatever the reason, his parting words had hurt me. Although I tried not to take them personally at the time, they are the kind of words you don't easily forget. Over the years when the *GMA* talent was asked to help promote that affiliate station, it was sometimes difficult to receive those requests with open arms.

This past year, when I left *GMA*, I certainly didn't want to burn any bridges, since I would be going back to promote my specials and my books. I definitely wanted to leave a good impression with the network as a team player, since I was still under contract with ABC for some time to come, so I was still part of that team. I wanted a receptive ear for any future projects I might want to produce. When they needed someone for a show, did I want them cringing and thinking, "Not her. Remember all the nasty things she said?" Did I want to be seen as full of sour grapes? Or did I want them to view me as an enthusiastic contributor to anything on which they might be working? I'm glad I chose not to burn a bridge.

RIGHT: *You can jump off a bridge—I've done it—just don't burn it!*

10

Know No Boundaries

What I admire in Columbus is
not his having discovered a
world, but his having gone to
search for it on the faith of an
opinion.

—Turgot

f Columbus had self-limits—if he had not dared to dream—the history of mankind would have been quite different. The lesson here: we cannot discover new oceans unless we have the courage to lose sight of the shore. We must dare to dream, to have adventures, and to know no boundaries.

Finding out who we are and what we want to do with our lives is our adventure. As with most adventures, we may sometimes have to brave the unknown to find what we seek. In pursuing our dreams, we must stretch and challenge ourselves. When we do, we may well be surprised at what strengths we have and at what we can accomplish. My mother must have told me a hundred times when I was growing up, "Don't wait for your ship to come in. You have to swim out to get it."

A few days after leaving *GMA*, I decided to make my own crossing of the Atlantic. I didn't have as much time as Columbus, so I took the Concorde. But I was definitely expanding my horizons. I had received an offer from Visa to go to Glasgow, Scotland, and give a speech at a convention on international travel. There would be seven thousand members of the American Society of Travel Agents attending. I had never been comfortable giving speeches in front of live audiences, and especially in front of seven thousand people! Okay, I know millions of people saw me every morning on *Good Morning America*, but when you're on television, you don't see the people on the other side of the camera. In the past, I had almost always turned these speech offers down. "I don't want to do them," I said, "because what could I possibly have to say that would actually be that compelling? And how do I know I'll be any good at giving speeches?"

They wanted me to speak for twenty-five minutes, which wasn't really that long. But to me it was an eon, because I was accustomed to thinking in terms of four-to-five-minute spots on *GMA*. Eight minutes on *GMA* had been practically an eternity. As I heard myself wondering if I had what it took to inspire people for close to a half hour, I had to stop myself.

Wait a minute! Maybe I *could* do it, after all. There was only one thing I knew for sure. If I didn't try, I'd never know.

Since it was a speech for travel agents, my first thought was, "What am I going to say to this group? What could we possibly have in common?" I took a deep breath, stopped my negative mind chatter, and began to reflect. I had grown up in a family where we had spent a great deal of time traveling. My father, as well as being a cancer specialist, was an avid pilot who flew all over the United States. My mom, my brother, and I often went with him. Perhaps these travel agents would be interested to know that even though my father was killed in a plane crash, my love of traveling and exploring the world was not diminished. Quite the contrary. My father would never have wanted his death to create fear in me or cause me to set up boundaries. He would have wanted me to keep on exploring the world, to learn life's lessons, and to make my mark. Okay! That was a good jumping-off point that I could use in my speech.

Then I remembered that I had spent my freshman college year as a part of World Campus Afloat, a college on-board an ocean liner, traveling to fifteen countries: Portugal, Spain, Morocco, Senegal, South Africa, Kenya, Tanzania, Uganda, India, Singapore, Thailand, Malaysia, Taiwan, China, and Japan. This unusual kind of world travel combined with study was another point of connection. I remembered that I skipped two grades in school, and I was only sixteen when I entered my freshman year of college on-board ship. Many of my mom's friends questioned her decision to allow me to go on this "'round the world" voyage at such a young age. But my mom wanted to expand my horizons, not to create boundaries. Okay, I had the title of my speech: "Know No Boundaries."

We all set up our own boundaries, our own self-imposed limits. It seemed so appropriate that in giving this speech, I would be shattering boundaries of my own. I had to let go of my fears that other people would disapprove of me. It reminded me of a famous ballplayer who was once asked how he managed to keep on playing when the crowd booed him. "I don't hear the boos," he explained, "because I don't hear the cheers." He had come to realize that if you depend too much on the opinions of others, you lose control of your own happiness. Feedback that comes from outside of yourself is not what counts. It's how you feel about yourself. I'm not suggesting that you ignore valuable feedback or that you don't acknowledge praise. Just don't let outside opinions take over your life.

If we rely on other people's opinions, we may be less inclined to take risks that are necessary for growth. Venturing out into new territory is almost impossible when we're worrying about how we will be perceived by others. Trying to do something beyond what we have already mastered is the only way to grow.

> *Never let the fear of striking out get in your way.*
>
> —*Babe Ruth*

If we're afraid of looking foolish, we'll never find out how great we could have been. No matter what happens, whether we achieve our goal this time or not, when we step out and take a risk, we never move backwards. Even failure is a positive step—often a necessary one along the path to our goal.

DREAM HIGHER DREAMS

Inspirational speaker Zig Ziglar says that we have a tendency to cut off our dreams, to not really boost ourselves up, because we're afraid of looking foolish. Or perhaps we're afraid of how great it's going to be. Instead, he recommends that we say, "I've had enough of this mediocrity in my life. I'm going to make the move." It's up to us to dream bigger dreams and to make those dreams come true. A friend once said to me, "You can't stuff a good life into a small dream."

What would you be doing with your life if there were no obstacles? If you could do whatever you wanted to do, be whatever you wanted to be, what would it be? What totally outrageous thing would you do if the outcome was guaranteed? Creating our future requires being aware of what we want from life. The only differences between us and the people who have the things we want are vision and belief. Dream, believe, feel the excitement, the intrigue, take the leap of faith—trust yourself enough to take the steps that will take you from where you are to where you want to be.

Everything we do starts with an idea, and dreams can only become realities if we acknowledge those ideas. One way to do this is to keep a dream list on which we write down, unedited, all the ideas that come to us. I keep my dream list in a journal that I sometimes call my Book of Brainstorms. When the creative window opens and a flurry of thoughts comes to me, I allow myself to dream and I write

> *The days come and go, but they say nothing, and if we do not use the gifts they bring, they carry them as silently away.*
>
> *—Ralph Waldo Emerson*

them all down in my book. I consider this book a door, one that I have built for myself to focus on my dreams and to actualize some of them on the other side.

Sometimes I give myself assignments that I write in my dream book. For instance, when it was time to start this book, I gave myself an assignment to go to the bookstore and research all the books I could find on change, transition, and risk-taking. I wanted to see what worked, which books drew me to pick them up and what made me want to put them back on the shelf. In this way, I could determine the needs of the marketplace as well as what I had to contribute.

My Book of Brainstorms not only has ideas but ways to achieve them.

For instance, one of my dreams is to do a daytime talk show, where I'd reconnect with my morning friends. I keep a list of people with whom I might enjoy working in the future: producers, directors, writers, and so on. As I passed through my transition, I gave myself an assignment to drop some of them a short note or give them a call. I wanted to let them know that I was starting on a new path. Then I made a note to myself to follow up by making appointments with some of these people to discuss possibilities. I pursued that one, and I met with a few people, just to talk and throw around ideas. Little by little, I was building self-confidence and my ideas for my future were taking form.

I may not do everything in my book, but that's not the point. I have come to discover that when we dream about things, we're acknowledging what we really want to do, even if at that moment, we don't have the courage to follow up. Maybe we'll read through our dream list next month or next year and we'll be ready to go forward on something we weren't yet prepared to do. The important thing is to keep the creative channels open, to allow ourselves to dream without editing, and write it all down.

There is great power in writing things down, because every journey begins with a single step. Many times, I've sat down with my dream list, read through it, and said, "That was a great idea. I think I'm ready to get started on it." The acknowledgment is the first step, and if it's something that's right for us, it somehow picks up its own momentum when the time is right.

The trick is not to censor or limit ourselves or create boundaries when we write down our dreams. I've spoken to others about keeping a dream list, and some of them have said, "So what should be on my list?" If you ask what you *should* write down, your list won't be an honest one. Instead of dreaming, you'll be trying to live up to someone else's expectations, and it will have nothing to do with you.

A dream list can be different things for different people. If raising children and taking care of a home is your primary role, your dream list might contain ideas that would make you a better mother or homemaker. You might list possible classes on gourmet cooking or decorating, house management or finances, or arts and crafts. Perhaps you want to join the PTA, attend the meetings, and one day find the courage to stand up and speak in front of a group of people.

> *One can never consent to creep When one feels an impulse to soar.*
>
> —*Helen Keller*

My most recent impulse to soar came when the U.S. Air Force agreed to take me flying in a U2 reconnaissance plane. I had heard that our air force pilots flew a most unusual plane at amazing heights—over seventy thousand feet—that could take detailed pictures of earth from the edge of the atmosphere. It sounded like the ultimate eye in the sky. Doing a story about this plane became a goal for *Behind Closed Doors*. However, this plane had been shrouded in secrecy since its inception in the fifties. In fact, its existence only came to the attention of the public in the sixties, when the Russians shot down U.S. Air Force pilot Francis Gary Powers. The Russians said he was spying on them from high altitudes over the Soviet Union. It took over three years of knocking on the door of the Pentagon to finally get the air force to let us behind the door of the plane called the "Dragon Lady."

The U2 was named the Dragon Lady for good reason. When everything's going right with the plane, the pilots say it's like dancing with a lady—flying higher and longer than any other plane in the world. It's also one of the most difficult planes to fly. With a 104-foot wingspan, it looks like the biggest glider you'll ever see. It has a monstrous jet engine that propels it to high altitudes. When flying seventy thousand feet above the earth, if the pilot goes ten knots too slow, the Dragon Lady will stall—ten knots too fast, and she'll break apart.

These unique planes canvass the skies, constantly taking pictures that are instantly downlinked to ground stations where they are monitored and analyzed by U.S. Air Force intelligence experts. This vital information can then be immediately transmitted to the president or secretary of defense in Washington, to field officers in combat areas, or to fighter-jet pilots who use the pictures for their attack strategies.

Like astronauts, U2 pilots must wear fully pressurized suits in order to survive at those high altitudes. Without them, the pilots' blood would boil when they ascended above sixty-three thousand feet. So when I found myself headed for Beale Air Force Base in northern California, where the U2 reconnaissance program is centered, I was quite apprehensive. Not so much about flying at high altitudes, but about how I would deal with wearing the pressurized suit. Have you ever taken a close look at the astronauts in their pressure suits and wondered what it would be like to be enclosed in one? Their helmets get locked down to the neck ring, and their gloves get locked to their cuffs. You're inside a cocoon where 100 percent pure oxygen is being pumped into your face mask, so that you hear and feel each breath you take. If you've ever been scuba diving, you know the sound. All I can say is that the thought freaked me out. I had read somewhere that bravery doesn't mean not being afraid. It simply means that you're the only one who knows you're afraid. Bravery is about facing your fear and dealing with it. As I headed to my latest adventure, I thought about being inside that second skin, closed off from the outside world. How would I deal with it? I hoped that in facing this challenge, I could turn my sense of fear into a sense of excitement. In retrospect, all that thinking probably fed my fear, but I kept it to myself and I dealt with it.

When I arrived at Beale, I went immediately into intensive training for my U2 flight. The moment of truth had arrived and I could feel my heart pounding. Having suffered for years with allergies and mild asthma, I

I never knew I was claustrophobic... until they locked down my helmet.

was concerned about my ability to breathe inside the cocoon. The cameras rolled as I suited up. Dozens of air force personnel were there looking on, and the pressure to make it through this training was enormous. If I didn't, all my producers, writers, and camera crews could pack up and go home. There would be no flight to the edge of space.

The heavy helmet reminded me of a full-head motorcycle helmet. As they fitted it over my head and locked it into the neck ring, I could sense that my heart rate and my breathing were changing. When they locked down the faceplate and turned on the oxygen, admittedly, a sense of panic took over. I tried to quiet my mind, to push out the panicked thoughts by utilizing every relaxation and breathing technique I'd ever learned. But the claustrophobia was almost too much. Several times I came very close to saying, "I'm sorry. I just can't do this." Thankfully, those thoughts were interrupted as the U2 crew prepared to lead me into the high-altitude chamber where we were to simulate a U2 flight.

About a dozen technicians and doctors watched me through the glass windows of the chamber to see how my body would function as they increased the altitude pressure. They first took me to 29,500 feet, then on up to 65,000 feet. Incidentally, they put a beaker of water inside the chamber with me so I could see the liquid boil when we reached 63,000 feet, the altitude at which my blood would boil if I were not in the pressure suit. Nice science project—but it only added fuel to my anxiety.

Then it was on to 75,000 feet, the highest altitude we would reach during the actual flight. They then brought me back down to 29,500 feet, where they turned off my oxygen supply so they could observe how I might deal with the possible symptoms of hypoxia (oxygen deprivation), commonly: dizziness, apprehension, tingling sensations in the fingers, blue lips, headache, euphoria, panic, and belligerence. I definitely felt apprehensive, in fact my breathing was becoming more shallow by the minute. The doctors outside the glass noted that my lips were turning blue. Well, at least it added some color to my face. Did I mention that you can wear no moisturizer, no makeup, no gel or hair spray? All of these oil-based products are highly combustible when mixed with 100 percent oxygen. Pure oxygen is also very drying, and my lips and mouth were so dry, I could barely swallow. "Are we done yet?" I asked.

"Oh," the doctor said, "there's another symptom—belligerence."

Everyone outside the glass laughed at the doctor's remark. My body was so taxed I couldn't muster the energy to join in.

It wasn't over yet. They then simulated a rapid decompression from 29,500 feet back up to 65,000 feet, to see how this drastic change in pressure would affect my ears. "Stay ahead of your ears," the technicians warned me. Most of us would hold our nose to pop our ears as the pressure changes, but ensconced inside your space helmet, you can't touch your face with your hands. (That gives new meaning to an itchy nose.) The whole thing took about an hour—one of the longest hours of my life. When I emerged from the high-altitude chamber, I was filled with mixed emotions. I wanted to fly high with these elite air force pilots, but the thought of being closed into that confining cocoon again was almost unbearable.

I spent the rest of the day learning about all the things that could go wrong with the plane and how to deal with each of these emergencies. I learned how to handle ejecting from the plane if I heard, "Bail out, bail out, bail out!" Next, it was virtual-reality parachute training. If you ejected at an altitude of seventy thousand feet, it would send you plummeting to earth at about 350 miles per hour. At fifteen thousand feet, your parachute would automatically deploy. At that point, you need the ability to guide yourself back to earth by pulling on one of two directional cords, just above your head. What a shame, my instructor said, to make it that far and not know how to guide yourself to a safe landing. I trained incessantly for the rest of the afternoon.

Another aspect of the unusual U2 design is that it's next to impossible for the pilots to clearly see the runway when landing. And after eight to twelve hours in the pressure suit, they're often so exhausted and dissipated, they can barely think or move. So each flight is assigned a "mobile" pilot who acts as the ground contact throughout the flight and talks the pilot down on final approach. This training day ended with my pilot, Lieutenant Colonel Mario Buda, and my mobile pilot, Major Brandon King, taking me to see the U2 in which I would be flying the next day. When I met Lieutenant Colonel Buda, I said to him, "It's a good thing your name is Buda, because it's gonna take me a lot of meditating to get through this flight."

As they pointed out the different gauges and knobs and dials in the cockpit, I began memorizing where each one was located. After the forty-five-minute session, they were amazed at my recall. I then confessed that I had to commit it all to memory, because I wore reading glasses and I couldn't really read the tiny writing next to each knob and dial.

I left the air force base that night for the hotel hoping that my anxiety would not keep me up all night. Happily, my exhaustion won the battle, but I did have a very vivid dream of my upcoming flight in absolute living color! The pilot and I bailed out at seventy thousand feet and I visualized the most unbelievable free fall to earth. The dream allowed me to practice everything I had learned that day. I maneuvered my parachute to a safe landing in a cow pasture. Once on the ground, as I struggled to get out of my pressure suit, I was overjoyed to look up and see Lieutenant Colonel Buda walking toward me. He had also survived.

We helped each other out of our cocoons. Standing there in our long johns, which the pilots wear under their pressure suits, we looked at each other and almost simultaneously said, "You don't see that happen every day." Kind of a John Wayne ending, I know, but a happy one. I later found out that throughout the years of the U2 program, two pilots *did* have to bail out at seventy thousand feet, and they *did* both survive.

For several days before and particularly that morning, I had to be extremely diligent about what I ate. I was told to avoid all gas-producing foods or carbonated beverages, because at high altitudes gas expands to five times its sea-level state. Just think about *that* bellyache for a minute! They also warned me against caffeine or any foods that might upset my stomach. Spicy burritos would not be on a U2 pilot's menu. The morning

*I felt like the
Pillsbury
Doughboy.*

225

of my flight, after toast and a plain egg omelette, I attended briefings at mission planning. I didn't let on to anyone how scared and tentative I was —that would mean admitting it out loud to myself and possibly increasing the level of concern of those around me, which could feed into my fear. Instead, each time I had a thought about this being scary, I immediately replaced "scary" with "exciting." Happily, all my psychological homework paid off when the time came to don my space cocoon. While it was still a weird and claustrophobic feeling, I was managing my fear.

Before each U2 flight, the pilots are required to breathe pure oxygen for at least an hour before takeoff. Lieutenant Colonel Buda recommended I try napping to pass the time. Oh, sure! Easier said than done. I tried to close my eyes and relax as much as possible. By keeping my mind busy with relaxation exercises, I couldn't focus on my fear, although those thoughts fought hard to get in. I had planned a number of different mind diversions. One was to imagine myself in a luxurious European spa where they offered these amazing oxygen treatments. I visualized the oxygen cleansing and purifying my ravaged sinus passages. I then saw it traveling down where it would open up the thousands of alveoli that line the lungs. As it restored my lungs to a healthier state, I thought, "No more asthma for me." With each inhalation, I visualized the oxygen flowing through my blood vessels, traveling out to rejuvenate my muscles and organs. How cool if it really *was* doing all of this! It did keep my mind occupied and my body as relaxed as I could have hoped. I distracted myself enough so that I lost track of time. It seemed like I had only been lying there about ten minutes when the technicians tapped me on the shoulder. It was time to go to the plane.

As they walked us out to the mobile units that would take us to the hangar, a technician followed a few steps behind me with a portable oxygen unit. This was my life support until they hooked us into the oxygen system in the aircraft. As I walked toward the U2, I saw my camera crews videotaping me and all the air force personnel scurrying around readying the plane, but I couldn't hear what any of them were saying. I could only hear my breath going in, out, in, out, in, out. It was surreal; I felt like I was in a world away from all of them. I felt like an astronaut.

Once inside the U2 cockpit, there was so much to do, so many hoses and tubes to connect, that my mind was distracted from my anxiety. They showed me my plastic water bottles and how to put the long tube through a tiny opening in my helmet and how I could direct it up to my mouth to take a sip. They showed me my food tubes, warning me that the chocolate pudding tubes sometimes exploded at high altitudes—not a pretty sight. The food choices had ranged from applesauce to peach cobbler to sloppy joes. They also showed me how to open the valve which allowed me to use my UCD (urinary containment device). Female pilots wear what looks like a sanitary pad with a plastic tube. The long johns that you wear under your pressure suit have a hole in the crotch, through which the plastic tubing fits. It then attaches to a tube in the bottom of the pressure suit. If you gotta go, you need to lean forward and release a valve, then increase the pressure in the suit. But when you do this, it blows the suit up so that you look like a giant Pillsbury Doughboy. Just like inflating a tire with air, the whole suit becomes so stiff, it takes an enormous amount of effort to just lift your hand, let alone bend forward and release a valve. You have to really need to go.

Okay. Everything was checked out, hooked up, and ready for takeoff. Then they lowered the canopy—one more chance to experience a little claustrophobia before leaving the ground. Everyone was watching, the cameras were rolling, flashes were going off, but still, all I heard was my breathing—in and out, in and out.

"Joan, turn your radio to UHF," said Lieutenant Colonel Buda, "and you'll hear air-traffic control." Finally, something else to hear besides my own breathing. I welcomed the noisy chatter from the tower. I also heard all of Lieutenant Colonel Buda's instructions.

Lock down your canopy.

Never let an adventure pass you by.

Roger, done.

Pressurize the canopy.

Roger, done. (Having memorized the cockpit, I quickly found each switch.)

As we taxied to the runway, Lieutenant Colonel Buda took me through the rest of the checklist and even let me call in the necessary requests to the tower. Once on the runway, he powered up our giant jet engines and then released the brakes.

We were off—soaring almost straight up at twelve thousand feet per minute. As quickly as we entered a thick cloud layer, we were out of it, passing by the last plane we would see on this ascent, a huge airliner coming in to land at San Francisco airport. The highest a commercial airliner flies is about 41,000 feet, and we were past that in minutes.

But when we neared sixty thousand feet, Lieutenant Colonel Buda's voice suddenly changed. For the first time, I heard concern and frustration. "Joan," he said, "we seem to have a problem. Failure of our AC generator. We're going to have to head back. I can climb a bit more as we turn around, but we're not going to be able to stay up here as planned. Sorry." He sounded so disappointed, but I must admit that my first impulse was to think, "What's so bad about that? We're up here, aren't we, at the edge of the atmosphere? And we got here in twenty-one minutes, which means we'll be back on the ground in close to the same time, and I can get out of this suit. That's having your cake and eating it, too." And anyway, I didn't really see why it was such a big deal being without AC. Of course, that's because I thought it meant air-conditioning. Then I learned it meant "alternating current," as in our power supply.

We headed back down. At fifty thousand feet, Lieutenant Colonel

Over northern California in my U2.

Buda said I could take over the airplane. Flying the U2, maintaining the correct altitude and speed, required so much focus and attention, I couldn't imagine having to do it for ten hours at a stretch. It was fun, but nerve-racking at the same time, and I was almost glad when, ten minutes later, he took back the controls.

But what happened next *was* a big deal. As Lieutenant Colonel Buda attempted to put down our landing gear, the gauge showed that the rear landing gear wasn't going down. Like a bicycle, the U2 has only two wheels. The prospect of having to land this plane without both wheels down was not something I wanted to think about. But planning for the worst was exactly what we had to do. We went through all of our emergency procedures. Then Lieutenant Colonel Buda declared an official emergency. The ground crew at Beale prepared for the worst. Lieutenant Colonel Buda explained that this was more likely a malfunction of the gauge than of the landing gear, but a pilot always has to prepare for the inevitability of a problem. The plan now was to do a low flyby at ten feet above the ground to let Beale technicians visually check to see if, in fact, our rear landing gear was locked in the "up" position as the gauge read, or if it was down.

As we soared back toward earth, I was surprised at how calm I remained in this crisis. Maybe I was just happy to have something else to think about besides my pressure suit. Lieutenant Colonel Buda was now constantly talking with those on the ground as we neared the runway at Beale. Doing a low flyby at jet speed was a bit unnerving, but not as unnerving as the sight of all the flashing lights of the emergency vehicles on the runway. As our mobile pilot "chased" beneath us, they gave us the good news that our landing gear was, in fact, down. We circled and came in for a landing. We were down and we were in one piece.

Safe on the ground, I thought, "I've been to the edge of space and back." I had faced fear and dealt with it. I remembered back to a commercial flight I had taken that prompted the same scare. The gauges had told the pilot that there were no hydraulics, so it would be impossible to put down the landing gear. That time, too, it proved to be only a malfunctioning gauge. The only difference was, I wasn't in the cockpit in a pressure suit. I was buckled into my seat, watching a movie.

While no one would invite an emergency, it was nice to know that taking my cue from Lieutenant Colonel Buda, an air force pilot trained to be calm in crisis, I had remained calm, too, focused on solutions. I was proud to have trained with such an elite, skilled, loyal, and dedicated group of people. I am heartened to know that they work daily to ensure our safety and our freedom. As for my new accomplishment, I realized that no one can predict what heights we may reach. Even we cannot know, until we spread our wings.

ALWAYS HAVE SOMETHING TO LOOK FORWARD TO

What we think about is what we become. In this way, life is a self-fulfilling prophecy. As I was growing up, my parents constantly told me, "Always have something to look forward to." Knowing that there are a variety of available choices can allow us to face an unknown future with excitement rather than fear.

I remember that shortly after leaving *GMA*, I was exploring a few ideas for my future with an agent who said, "Expand your dreams and then put yourself in the vicinity of those dreams." He, too, was giving me the same lesson that I'd been given as a child: always have something to look forward to.

Don't postpone your life. Don't say, "Someday I'll do something

> *We all live in suspense, from day to day, from hour to hour; in other words, we are the hero of our own story.*
>
> — *Mary McCarthy*

exciting, someday I'll be happy. I'll just wait until it gets a little easier." We must recognize that life will always bring change and we'll always have challenges, and they won't always be easy. But it can seem more manageable if we accept that obstacles are an integral part of our path.

> *Far away, there in the sunshine, are my highest aspirations. I may not reach them, but I can look up and see their beauty, believe in them, and try to follow where they lead.*
>
> *—Louisa May Alcott*

Too many people try to softly tiptoe down that path, so they can arrive at death safe and sound. But I believe our gift in life is to make our path the best and the most fulfilling it can be. It's never too late to feed our thirst for life and kindle our spirit for adventure. In so doing, we can find our gift, and in giving it to others, we will find self-fulfillment.

As soon as you start dreaming bigger dreams and go after them, be sure to revel in your accomplishments, and I mean that literally. Children have a refrigerator on which to proudly display their accomplishments. Doctors and CEOs have their office walls filled with awards and degrees. So why shouldn't we do the same? Make yourself a victory wall somewhere in your house. Okay, yes, I do have pictures of myself in a really cool Navy SEAL camouflage getup, learning to use an M-60. I have a poster of me climbing the Mendenhall Glacier in Alaska. And yes, I have a poster of me jumping off the bungee bridge in Queenstown, New Zealand.

But the photos that mean the most to me are those of me with my girls. They are my greatest accomplishment, my greatest challenge, and my greatest source of pride. I also love the one of me with Jeff, because it represents my ability to open up my heart and let down those self-protective walls.

Chronicle your accomplishments, big and small. Perhaps a shot of you in front of the PTA or a local charity group, making a difference. What about a shot of you golfing or playing tennis with an oh-so-professional look to your swing? I have a shot of me jumping my horse where I really look like I know what I'm doing. I love that one. So have someone take a picture of you amid a garden you've created or in a room you've decorated. Don't forget a photo with your family to remind you of the wonderful life you've helped create. Put them up in a place in your house that you'll see often. The visual reminders of your accomplishments will inspire you to new heights.

WRITE YOUR OWN STORY

When I first stepped out into my new life, I felt the added pressure of trying to replicate something as spectacular as *GMA*. Then I realized that if I just listened to my own hopes and desires, stayed true to them, and pursued them, I would create a different yet fulfilling chapter. I saw that in life what sometimes appears to be the end is often a new beginning. And a little push in the right direction can make a big difference. Life's bends, at times, can be frustrating or disheartening, but they need not defeat us. Our will to survive and evolve is greater than any stumbling block. We must remember that it's okay to feel vulnerable, threatened, and defenseless during change. However, overdependence on "life as it is" renders us unwilling to think new thoughts, dare new actions, or take new risks.

Coming to terms with our changing world is an ongoing negotiation. Our only guarantees are that life will change, our circumstances will change, and we will change. And quite likely, the tools and techniques that served us in the past may not serve us on the road ahead. So it's important to keep an open, flexible, and creative mind. Wondering, questioning, exploring—this is what growth, self-fulfillment, and self-improvement are all about. If we never ask new questions, we'll never get new answers. If

Some of the photos
on my victory wall.

we don't explore new paths, we'll never make new discoveries. Sometimes we need to go out on a limb because that's where we find the fruit.

The things we value usually come from stretching ourselves and sometimes taking risks. A mapped-out, predictable, uneventful life may seem safer. But there are so many paths to go down and explore, we just have to be willing to venture around the bend. If we're resistant to change, then it will be difficult to embrace something we've never done before. As our reality changes, and it always will, our task is to adapt—to let go of something old and reach out for something new. I'm glad I took the time to make it all the way around the bend and to let go of the old. I'm excited about the new path that lies ahead and the opportunity to once again reinvent myself.

Life's transactions don't always have to be so traumatic unless we resist them. So let's be wise in this business called life. Let's renegotiate our reality when it's necessary. When in pursuit of new experiences, we must be careful not to set boundaries, but rather to keep our aim high. If we shoot for the moon, even if we miss it, we'll still be landing somewhere among the stars.

> *Don't give up. Keep going. There is always a chance that you will stumble onto something terrific. I have never heard of anyone stumbling over anything while he was sitting down.*
>
> *—Ann Landers*

It's important, too, to reach out and touch others. I usually find the result is the enrichment of my own life. So listen to your own aspirations, believe in yourself, and do the things you thought you couldn't do. Speak up at that meeting, write that letter, communicate your feelings, offer your ideas and your assistance, and ask for help when you're overworked and carrying more than your share. And no less important, remember to make time for fun, relaxation, and exciting moments.

When I look back at my life, what will I most remember? What stories will I tell my grandchildren? Do I really think I'll remember being a certain dress size? Or will I recall taking a special trip with my daughters, exploring new places, perhaps a ski run well navigated or a mountain peak challenged. Each day, I want to live my life in such a way that I might have fulfilling and exciting memories. I want to remain open to new challenges—to continue to test myself outside my comfort zone. And they don't all have to be adrenaline journeys. So let's not get caught up in analyzing and rating our dreams or comparing them to others. We don't need to be the president of a big company or run a marathon or be an astronaut. There are many ways to find our self-esteem and self-fulfillment, ways that keep us growing—oh yes, and changing.

I look at my life as an unfinished story. I can give it direction, start new chapters, and fill it with extraordinary experiences. I can make it more fulfilling, more exciting, and more meaningful. As I finish writing this book, I am beginning a new chapter in my life. I'm tossing my hat back into the ring and going for my dream. I've sold my daytime talk show idea to Telepictures, the syndicated television division of Warner Bros.

By following the positive principles I laid out in this book, I have created the opportunity to realize my dream—a chance to write my own story.

The same can be true for you. We all write our own life story. Your story is determined not so much by what life brings to you, but by the attitude and passion and curiosity you bring to life. As your story unfolds, new characters can enter and leave. It will be full of unexpected twists and turns. And whether these bends in the road bring comedy or tragedy, boredom or excitement to your story, you can write whatever you want on your future pages.

What will come next? You're writing the story. It will unfold as you create it.

Photography Credits

All photographs are from Joan Lunden's personal collection, except for those listed here.

Bends in the Road illustration: Phil Kimmelman. xiv: © Andrew Eccles/ABC, Inc. 7: © Ida Mae Astute/ABC, Inc. 12: Leo Cullum © 1993 from *The New Yorker* collection. All Rights Reserved. 15: © Andrew Eccles/ABC, Inc. 22: © Andrew Eccles/ABC, Inc. 26: © ABC, Inc. 30: © Steve Fenn/ABC, Inc. 31: © Steve Fenn/ABC, Inc. 33: © Steve Fenn/ABC, Inc. 34: © Craig Sjodin/ABC, Inc. 34: © Craig Sjodin/ABC, Inc. 35: © Jill Alpert Seigerman. 36: © Craig Sjodin/ABC, Inc. 36: © David Goldman. 39: Courtesy of *TV Guide*. 41: © 1997 Time, Inc. 42: © 1998 Warner Bros. All Rights Reserved. 43: © Andrew Eccles/ABC, Inc. 44: © Steve Fenn/ABC, Inc. 55: © *The Late Show with David Letterman.* Courtesy of Worldwide Pants Incorporated. 56: © Steve Fenn/ABC, Inc. 62: © Steve Fenn/ABC, Inc. 63: © ABC, Inc. 66: © Ida Mae Astute/ABC, Inc. 67: © Ida Mae Astute/ABC, Inc. 68: © Ida Mae Astute/ABC, Inc. 69: © Ida Mae Astute/ABC, Inc. 69: © Ida Mae Astute/ABC, Inc. 70: © Ida Mae Astute/ABC, Inc. 71: © Ida Mae Astute/ABC, Inc. 72: © Ida Mae Astute/ABC, Inc. 74: © Ida Mae Astute/ABC, Inc. 75: © Ida Mae Astute/ABC, Inc. 76: © Outline Press Syndicate, Inc./Timothy White. 78: © Steve Fenn/ABC, Inc. 89: © 1996 New Life Entertainment, Inc./Simon Bruty. 93: © Outline Press Syndicate, Inc./Timothy White. 95: © ABC, Inc. 96: © Brian Fitzgerald/ABC, Inc. 98: © 1998 Glamour Shots. 99: © ABC, Inc. 101: © Terry Ashe/ABC, Inc. 102: Courtesy of U.S. Navy. 102: © Michael Yarish/ABC, Inc. 103: © Kristen Barry. 104: © Terry Ashe/ABC, Inc. 105: © Terry Ashe/ABC, Inc. 106: © Terry Ashe/ABC, Inc. 106: ©Terry Ashe/ABC, Inc. 109: Courtesy of Bally's Las Vegas, "Jubilee" show. Costume designer: Bob Mackie. 110: © Republic Entertainment, Inc./Timothy White. 115: © Brian Fitzgerald/ABC, Inc. 116: © Brian Fitzgerald/ABC, Inc. 117: © Brian Fitzgerald/ABC, Inc. 118: © Brian Fitzgerald/ABC, Inc. 125: © Vicki Miceli. 125: © Vicki Miceli. 127: © Brian Fitzgerald/ABC, Inc. 127: © Brian Fitzgerald/ABC, Inc. 128: © Andrew Eccles/ABC, Inc. 130: © Outline Press Syndicate, Inc./Sam Jones. 133: © Ida Mae Astute/ABC, Inc. 134: ©1995 Figge Photography, Inc. 135: © New Life Entertainment, Inc./Simon Bruty. 137: © Outline Press Syndicate, Inc./Sam Jones. 142: *Top right:* © Outline Press Syndicate, Inc./EJ Camp. *Bottom left:* © Bob Tarr, Cincinnati, Ohio. 145: © New Life Entertainment, Inc./Simon Bruty. 146: © New Life Entertainment, Inc./Simon Bruty. 149: © Steve Fenn/ABC, Inc. 153: © New Life Entertainment, Inc. Simon Bruty. 155: © Ida Mae Astute/ABC, Inc. 162: © Andrew Eccles/ABC, Inc. 165: © Timothy White/ABC, Inc. 166: © Ann Underwood. 167: © New Life Entertainment, Inc./Pablo Ramirez. 177: © Steve Fenn/ABC, Inc. 184: ©Jim Jackson. 187: © 1998